EXERCISES
IN
FRENCH PROSE
AND
FREE COMPOSITION

EXERCISES IN
FRENCH PROSE
AND
FREE COMPOSITION

BY

C. W. WORDSWORTH, M.A., L. ès L.

Late Exhibitioner of Trinity College, Cambridge
Late Assistant Master at Sherborne School
Author of 'Modern French Syntax and Composition'

CAMBRIDGE
AT THE UNIVERSITY PRESS
1938

CAMBRIDGE
UNIVERSITY PRESS

University Printing House, Cambridge CB2 8BS, United Kingdom

Cambridge University Press is part of the University of Cambridge.

It furthers the University's mission by disseminating knowledge in the pursuit of education, learning and research at the highest international levels of excellence.

www.cambridge.org
Information on this title: www.cambridge.org/9781316601747

First published 1938
First paperback edition 2015

A catalogue record for this publication is available from the British Library

ISBN 978-1-316-60174-7 Paperback

PREFACE

This book is intended to provide a series of exercises in French Prose and Free Composition for the use of candidates taking the following examinations:

Cambridge Local Junior Certificate.
Northern Universities Joint Matriculation.
London Matriculation and General School Examination.
Cambridge Local School Certificate.
Oxford Local School Certificate.

The book is divided into four Sections.

Section I consists of an outline of French Syntax, to which frequent reference is made in the footnotes to the Exercises. This outline is, in the main, a collection of examples of the rules for French Syntax, with which the pupil will have to deal when he or she is translating the passages set for translation into French in Section II.

Section II is divided into three parts:

(*a*) Examination papers.
(*b*) Anecdotes.
(*c*) Original English passages (mostly from modern authors and including extracts from *Punch*).

In each of these three parts the Exercises are roughly graded in order of difficulty, and nearly all the Exercises have footnotes. These footnotes will, I hope, be found valuable as showing how to surmount the many and various difficulties, which arise in the translation of even the simplest English into good French.

Before deciding on the final form of the Anecdotes and Original English passages in Section II, I took the precaution of adapting and simplifying the English and I then translated the simplified versions into French. The final wording of the English text was based on my French translations as amended and revised by the following French teachers, to whom I tender my acknowledgements and best thanks:

Mademoiselle E. R. Monteil, until lately professeur at the Institut Français de Londres.

Monsieur E. Renoir, professeur agrégé au Lycée Hoche, Versailles.

Monsieur L. E. Génissieux, Director of the London Bureau of the Office National des Universités et Écoles Françaises.

Through the kind offices of Professor Desseignet of the University of Reading I have also been able to obtain the assistance of Monsieur Louis Pallier of Châteauneuf, Puy-de-Dôme, who is an expert in the translation of English into French. Also, through the kindness of Monsieur Charvet, lecturer in French at Corpus Christi College, Cambridge, I have been able to refer some doubtful points to Monsieur I. Macé, of Paris, who has a good knowledge of English as well as French.

Section III consists of Exercises in Free Composition, preceded by special vocabularies which are intended to be learnt by heart.

The three forms of Free Composition Exercises which are most in use at examinations appear to be

(1) Sujets de Composition.

(2) Continuation Exercises.

(3) Expansion Exercises or Canevas à développer.

I have therefore provided more exercises in these branches of Composition than in the less common forms of Conversation and Letter Writing.

In Section IV will be found a full General Vocabulary to all the Exercises in Section II and the Continuation Exercises in Section III. It has been my aim to make this book as self-contained as possible, and I hope that, with the help of the outline of French Syntax and the General Vocabulary, the pupil will have all the material necessary for the translation of the Exercises.

I wish to express my acknowledgements and thanks to the following examination bodies for permission to reprint extracts from papers set by them:

(1) The Local Examinations Syndicate of the University of Cambridge for permission to reprint extracts from Cambridge Local Junior and School Certificate papers.

(2) The Joint Matriculation Board of the Northern Universities for permission to reprint extracts from papers set in Northern Universities Matriculation and School Certificate papers.

(3) The Senate of the University of London for permission to reproduce extracts from the papers set for the Matriculation and General Schools Examinations.

(4) The Delegates of the Oxford Local Examinations Board for permission to reprint extracts from the Oxford Local School Certificate papers.

I also wish to express my thanks to the following publishers and authors for permission to reprint short extracts from works of which they hold the copyright:

In Section II (*b*) (Anecdotes) to the Universal Publications Co. for Nos. IX, XI, XIII, XVI, XX, to the Richards Press for Nos. X, XVIII, and to Messrs Davis and Moughton Ltd., Birmingham, for Nos. V, VI and VII.

In Section II (*c*) (Original passages) to the Proprietors of *Punch* for Nos. I–VI, XI–XII, XV, XIX–XX, XXIV–XXV, XXVII, XXXIV, XLIII–XLIV, XLVI, XLIX; to Messrs Methuen and Co. Ltd. and Mr A. E. Milne for Nos. VII–IX, XXXV–XXXVII; to Messrs J. W. Arrowsmith (London) Ltd. for Nos. XVI–XVIII; to Messrs Samuel French Ltd. for Nos. XXI–XXIII; to Messrs Collins and Co. for Nos. XXIX–XXX, XLII; to Messrs Chapman and Hall for Nos. XLVIII, L, LIII; to Messrs Chatto and Windus for Nos. LI, LII; to Messrs William Heinemann and Co. and Major the Hon. Maurice Baring for No. XXVI; to Messrs Macmillan and Co. and Major Dodgson for No. XLII; to Messrs Methuen and Co. and Mr Philip Carr for No. LV; and to the Oxford University Press for Nos. XXVII, XXXI–XXXIII.

It is of course understood that most of the above passages have been simplified and adapted for translation into French.

Finally I wish to thank the acting Librarian of the Hastings Town Library for help in obtaining books which, in one or two cases, are out of print.

C. W. WORDSWORTH

St Leonards-on-Sea

ERRATA

p. 6, §8 (*b*) read Combien y en a-t-il?

p. 18, §64 (*b*) delete daigner de condescend to.

p. 181 read **condescend,** *daigner* (+ inf. without prep.).

CONTENTS

SECTION I

OUTLINE OF FRENCH SYNTAX

SECTION II

PASSAGES FOR FRENCH PROSE

SECTION III

FREE COMPOSITION

SECTION IV

Section I

OUTLINE OF FRENCH SYNTAX

(To which reference is made in the footnotes to the exercises)

THE DEFINITE ARTICLE

§ 1.

(*a*)	Le premier juin	**On** the first of June
	Le vingt-et-un décembre	**On** the twenty-first of December
(*b*)	Le jour de Noël	**On** Christmas Day
	Le jour de l'ouverture	**On** the day of the opening
	Le matin	**In** the morning
	L'après-midi	**In** the afternoon
	Le soir	**In** the evening, **on** the evening (of)
	La nuit	**At** night
(*c*)	Il viendra samedi	He will come **on Saturday**
	Il vient le dimanche	He comes **on Sundays**
(*d*)	La France	France
	L'Angleterre	England
	but	
	En France	In *or* to France
	De France	From France
	En Angleterre	In *or* to England
	D'Angleterre	From England
(*e*)	À Londres	To *or* in London
	À Paris	To *or* in Paris
(*f*)	Le français	French
	but	
	En français	In French
	Parler français	Speak French
(*g*)	Le jeune Henri	Young Henry
	La petite Marie	Little Mary

(*h*)	Il leva le bras	He raised **his** arm
	Elle secoua la tête	She shook **her** head
	Ils levèrent **la** tête	They raised **their** heads
	Il se grattait la tête	He was scratching **his** head
	On lui frotta les mains	They rubbed **his** (or **her**) hands
	Je lui glissai une pièce dans la main	I slipped a coin into **his** hand
(*i*)	Il entra la canne à la main	He entered **with** his stick in his hand
(*j*)	L'un d'eux	One of them

OMISSION OF THE INDEFINITE ARTICLE

§ 2.

(*a*)	Il est fermier	He is **a** farmer
	Il devint officier	He became **an** officer
(*b*)	Il fut vendu comme esclave	He was sold as **a** slave
	Acheter comme cadeau	Buy as **a** present
(*c*)	Sortir sans chapeau	Go out without **a** hat

(*a*) PARTITIVE ARTICLE (*du, de la, de l', des*)
(*b*) TO (*h*) PARTITIVE AND OTHER USES OF *DE*

§ 3.

(*a*)	Bien des choses	Many things
	Bien des gens	Many people
	Bien des fois	Many times
	Bien des années	Many years

(*Des* is here the Partitive Article intensified by the adverb *bien*.)

(*b*)	D'excellent vin	(Some) excellent wine
	De bons amis	Good friends
	D'autres fois	(At) other times

(*De* instead of Partitive Article before adjective preceding noun.)

(*c*)	Il n'y a pas de place	There is no room
	Il n'y a pas eu de vol	There has been no theft
	N'a-t-il pas d'enfants?	Hasn't he any children?
	Il n'y a plus de papier	There is no more paper

De instead of Partitive Article after a negative.)

But

Il **n'y a que du pain**	There is only bread

(Because *ne...que* is an affirmative expression.)

(*d*) Tant de pain	So much bread
Tant de fleurs	So many flowers
Tant de monde	So many people
Trop de monde	Too many people
Un peu de pain	A little bread
Peu de pain	Only a little bread
Peu de nouvelles	Little news
Si peu de monde	So few people
Très peu de maisons	Very few houses
(*e*) Quelque chose de bon	Something good
Rien de remarquable	Nothing remarkable
(*f*) Un drôle de garçon	A funny (or odd) fellow
Ce sont de drôles de gens	They are funny people
Quel drôle de manteau !	What an odd cloak !
Quelle drôle d'idée !	What a funny idea !
(*g*) La plupart **des** gens le **font**	Most people do it
La plupart de mes compagnons	Most of my companions
(*h*) Une bouteille pleine d'encre	A bottle full of ink
Couvert de papier	Covered with paper
Remplir d'eau	To fill with water
Se passer de domestique	Do without a servant

In (*g*) and (*h*) *de* is a preposition.

POSITION OF ADJECTIVES

§ 4. (*a*) Before nouns.

Short and common adjectives:

beau	haut	meilleur	vaste
bon	jeune	moindre	vieux
gentil	joli	petit	vilain
gros	mauvais	sot	

(*b*) After nouns.

Adjectives of nationality, religion, shape and colour, e.g. *français, catholique, rond, rouge.*

The normal position of the adjective in French is after the noun. This position serves to distinguish a person or animal or thing from others of the same class, e.g. *un cheval noir* as distinguished from *un cheval blanc.* It is therefore particularly appropriate to descriptive epithets.

(*c*) When two adjectives govern the same noun the above order is generally observed.

e.g. Une gentille petite fille
but Une petite fille intelligente

Une jolie petite maison
but Une grande maison laide
A large ugly house.

Adjectives of one syllable tend to precede the noun, when the noun is qualified by a second adjective.

e.g. De *longues* routes étroites
Long narrow roads

(*d*) Superlative use.

Un homme des plus intéressants
A most interesting man

Une histoire des plus amusantes
A most amusing story

NEGATIVES

§ 5. Position of Negatives.

Ne pas, ne plus, ne rien and *ne jamais* before Present and Perfect Infinitive.

e.g. Il m'a dit de ne pas venir
Je regrette de ne pas l'avoir vu

§ 6. Negatives.

(*a*) Il **ne** lui restait **plus** d'argent — He had no money left
Il **n'y a plus** de fiacres — There are no cabs nowadays
Vous **ne** le verrez **jamais plus** — You will never see him again
Vous **n'**en trouverez **guère** — You will scarcely find any

(*b*) Je **n'**ai **aucune** intention de répondre
I have no intention of replying
Aucun de mes amis **n'**a répondu
None of my friends has replied

(*c*) Est-ce que **personne d'autre n'**en a pris?
Didn't anyone else have any?

(*d*) Il **n'**avait **ni** parents **ni** amis — He had no relatives or friends
Ni son père **ni** sa mère **ne** le savaient
Neither his father nor his mother knew
Sans souliers **ni** bas — Without shoes or stockings
Sans rien dire — Without saying anything

(*e*) Il **ne** l'a pas fait **non plus** — He hasn't done it either

(*f*) Il **ne** fit **que** crier — {He only (*or* merely) shouted / He did nothing but shout}
Il **ne** put **que** sangloter — He could do nothing but sob

(*g*) Je **ne** saurais vous dire — I couldn't tell you
Je **n'**ose le faire — I daren't do it

§ 7. Redundant NE.

(*a*) Il est plus âgé qu'il **ne** paraît — He is older than he looks
Il est plus heureux ici qu'il **ne** l'était chez vous
He is happier here than he was with you

(*b*) Il y a longtemps que je **ne** l'ai vu
{It is a long time since I have seen him / I have not seen him for a long time}
Il y avait plus de trois ans que je **ne** l'avais vu
{It was more than three years **since** I had seen him / I had not seen him **for** more than three years}

Ne...pas is sometimes used, instead of *ne* alone, in this type of sentence.

PERSONAL PRONOUNS

§ 8.	(*a*)	On me l'a dit	I have been told so
	(*b*)	Il en est le propriétaire	He is the owner of it
		Il en est très content	He is very pleased with it
		Il en a peur	He is afraid of it (*or* them)
		J'en ai vu plusieurs	I have seen several
		Je vais en acheter un	I am going to buy one
		J'en ai vu un gris	I have seen a grey one
		Combien y a-t-il?	How many are there?
		Il y en a quatre	There are four
		Il n'y en a pas	There is / There are } none There isn't / There aren't } any

DISJUNCTIVE PRONOUNS

§ 9. (*a*) After prepositions.

Avec eux (*or* elles)	With them
Sans eux (*or* elles)	Without them
Il courut vers moi	He ran towards me
Il regarda autour de lui	He looked round him

(*b*) In comparisons.
Personne n'est plus brave que lui
No one is braver than he

(*c*) Ma sœur et moi nous sortions tous les matins
My sister and I went out every morning

Lui et sa femme sont venus nous voir
He and his wife came to see us

INTERROGATIVE AND EXCLAMATORY PRONOUNS

§ 10.	(*a*)	Qu'est-ce que c'est que ça?	What's that?
	(*b*)	Quel plaisir !	What a pleasure !
		Quel dommage !	What a pity !

(Note omission of article in French.)

RELATIVE PRONOUNS

§ 11. (*a*) The relative must be expressed in French when omitted in English.

La plume **que** je vous ai donnée	The pen I gave you
L'hôtel **dont** vous parlez	The hotel you speak of

(*b*) **Un jour que**	**One day when, one day while**
Le jour où	**The day when**

Uses of quoi

§ 12. (*a*) *Relative*

À quoi il répondit — To which he replied

(*b*) *Interrogative*

Je ne sais pas de quoi vous riez
I do not know what you are laughing at

DEMONSTRATIVE PRONOUNS

§ 13. (*a*) Je ne suis pas bien portant **ces temps-ci**
I have not been very well lately

Ce jour-là — On that day

(*b*) **Ce** pauvre André ! — Poor André !

§ 14.

Celui-ci } This one, *or*	Celui-là } That one, *or*
Celle-ci } the latter	Celle-là } the former

Demonstrative and Relative

§ 15.

Celui qui	He who *or* the one which
Celle qui	She " " " " "

Ce qui, ce que, etc.

§ 16. (*a*) Vous y trouverez ce qu'il vous faut
You will find what you want

Ce qu'il vous faut c'est...
What you want is...

(*b*) Je ne sais pas ce qu'il y a
I don't know what is the matter
Je me demande ce qu'il a fait
I wonder what he has done

(*c*) Je ne sais pas ce que c'est
I don't know what it is
Il ne sait pas ce que **c'est** que les passages cloutés
He doesn't know what pedestrian crossings **are**

(*d*) 'Which', in apposition to a sentence:
Il avait manqué le train, ce qui était ennuyeux
He had missed the train, which was annoying
Il me pria de m'asseoir, ce que je fis
He begged me to sit down, which I did

(*e*) *Qui* is generally used instead of *ce qui* after *voilà*:
Voilà qui est merveilleux! That's splendid!

INDEFINITE ADJECTIVES AND PRONOUNS

§ 17.

(*a*) Le même roi — The same king
Le roi même — The king himself

(*b*) *On* is often used to avoid the passive.
e.g. On fera un exemple — An example shall be made
On avait envoyé un domestique — A servant had been sent
On lui apporta une lettre — A letter was brought to him
On demanda à mon père — My father was asked
On lui avait enlevé son couteau
His knife had been taken away from him

(*c*) Quelques-uns de ces messieurs — Some of these gentlemen
Quelqu'un d'entre vous a-t-il des allumettes?
Has anyone got any matches?

(*d*) Translation of 'such'.
Une telle femme — Such a woman
Une si belle femme — Such a beautiful woman / So beautiful a woman

(*e*) *Pareil* is generally used in an unfavourable sense.

Une chose pareille	Such an (extraordinary) thing
(*f*) L'auto partit telle une flèche	The car shot off like an arrow

(*g*) *Tout* meaning 'quite' is invariable except before an adjective or participle beginning with a consonant or *h* aspirate.

Tout étonnée	Quite astonished
Tout heureuse (*h* mute)	Quite happy
but Toute surprise	Quite surprised
Toute honteuse (*h* aspirate)	Quite ashamed

VERB + PREPOSITION + NOUN

§ 18. Privative Verbs. Accusative of the thing. Dative of the person.

Le voleur **lui a pris** son argent
The robber has taken his money from him
L'homme **lui avait volé** sa bourse
The man had stolen his purse from him }
The man had robbed him of his purse }

§ 19. Other privative verbs taking the same construction:

acheter, buy   *cacher*, hide   *emprunter*, borrow

§ 20. The Passive of these verbs is expressed by using *on* with the active.

e.g. On lui a pris son argent	His money has been taken from him
On lui avait enlevé son épée	His sword had been taken away from him

§ 21. Verbs with preposition in English but not in French.

Regarder, look at	*Payer*, pay for
Chercher, look for	*Attendre*, wait for

e.g. Combien avez-vous payé ce chapeau?
How much did you pay for this hat?
Je l'ai payé cinquante francs
I paid fifty francs for it.

§ 22. Verbs with preposition in French, but not in English.

Il entra dans le salon	He entered the drawing-room
Il répondit à la question	He answered the question

§ 23. Construction with *demander*.

Il demanda un billet	He asked for a ticket
Il demanda à son père	He asked his father

Il demanda au garçon un verre de vin blanc
He asked the waiter for a glass of white wine

Passive. On demanda au prisonnier — The prisoner was asked

C'EST AND *IL EST*

§ 24. Est-ce le boulanger? — Oui, c'est le boulanger
Is it the baker? — Yes, it is the baker

§ 25. Il est difficile de savoir tant de choses
„ impossible „ „ „ „
It is difficult to know so many things
„ impossible „ „ „ „

§ 26. Colloquial use of *c'est*, instead of *il est*, in similar phrases.

Ce n'est pas poli de crier — It is not polite to shout

§ 27. *IL Y A*

Il y a	There is, there are	Y a-t-il?	Is there? Are there?
Il y aura	There will be	Y aura-t-il?	Will there be?
Il y avait	There was, there were	Il y eut	There was *or* were (meaning 'there followed', 'there came about')
Il y a eu	There has been, there have been	Il y avait eu	There had been

Negative: Il n'y a pas. Negative interrogative: N'y a-t-il pas?

§ 28. INTERROGATIVE WORD ORDER

Pourquoi Monsieur Dupont écrit-il une lettre?
Why is Monsieur Dupont writing a letter?
Pourquoi votre père a-t-il dit cela?
Why did your father say that?

§ 29. AFFIRMATIVE AND NEGATIVE EXPRESSIONS

Je crois que oui	I think so
Je ne crois pas	I don't think so

CONJUNCTIONS

§ 30. aussi with inversion of verb and pronoun.

Aussi fut-elle toute surprise...
So she was quite surprised...

§ 31. puisque.

(1) Puisque vous le dites, il faut vous croire
Since you say so, we must believe you

(2) With main clause suppressed:
Eh, bien, puisque vous insistez...
Well, since you insist... (I will do it)

§ 32. peut-être.

(1) Il est peut-être rentré chez lui
Perhaps he has returned home

(2) Peut-être qu'il reviendra
Perhaps he will come back

(3) With inversion of pronoun and verb:
Peut-être s'est-il fait mal
Perhaps he has hurt himself

§ 33. que is used to avoid repetition of *comme*, *quand* and *lorsque*.

Comme / Quand / Lorsque } il faisait beau **et que** tout le monde voulait sortir

As / When } it was fine **and** everyone wanted to go out

§ 34. Au moment où il entrait Just as he was going in

§ 35. Participial Phrase to replace conjunction.

Le déjeuner fini When lunch was over

§ 36. Phrases to replace conjunctions.

À mon réveil	When I woke up
Dès sa rentrée	As soon as he returned home
Dès son embarquement	As soon as he went on board

INDICATIVE

§ 37. *Present.*

(*a*) Depuis combien de temps **attendez-vous**?
For how long **have** you **been** waiting?

J'attends depuis une demi-heure
I have been waiting for half an hour

Il **est** absent depuis deux mois
He **has been** away **for** (the last) two months

(*b*) Il est en train de dîner
He is having his dinner

§ 38. *Imperfect.*

(*a*) Il **attendait** depuis une demi-heure
He **had been** waiting **for** half an hour

Il **était** absent depuis deux mois
He **had been** away **for** two months

(*b*) Il était en train de dîner
He was having his dinner

(*c*) Tous les matins il **sortait** à neuf heures
Every morning he **would** (*or* **used to**) **go out** at nine o'clock

§ 39. *Future.*

Je vous reverrai, quand je **reviendrai**
I shall see you again, when I **come back**

Quand vous **sortirez**, prenez votre parapluie
When you **go out**, take your umbrella

§ 40. *Future Perfect.*

Quand vous **aurez fini** votre travail, venez me voir
When you **have finished** your work, come and see me

§ 41. *Future in the Past.*

Il promit de venir me voir, lorsqu'il **reviendrait**
He promised to come and see me, when he **returned**

§ 42. *Future Perfect in the Past.*

Il m'a dit de venir, lorsque j'**aurais fini** mon travail
He told me to come, when **I had** finished my work

§ 43. *Past Definite.*

Il y **eut** un temps d'arrêt	There was a pause
Il **eut** un instant d'hésitation	He hesitated for a moment
Le porteur **eut** une idée	The porter had an idea
Il y **resta** longtemps	He remained there a long time

§ 44. *Second Pluperfect.*

Lorsqu'il **eut fini** de parler, on l'applaudit
When he had finished speaking, he was applauded

Il n'**eut** pas plus tôt **fini** de parler qu'on l'applaudit
He had no sooner finished speaking than he was applauded

§ 45. Examples of Conditional Clauses.

(*a*) S'il **vient**, je vous le **dirai**
If he comes I will tell you

(*b*) Si je le **savais**, je vous le **dirais**
If I knew, I would tell you

S'il **venait**, je vous **préviendrais**
If he should come I would inform you

(*c*) Si je l'**avais su**, je vous l'**aurais dit**
If I had known, I would have told you

§ 46. *Si* meaning 'if' cannot be used with a Future Indicative. In many cases *vouloir* may be used.

e.g. Si vous voulez venir demain
If you will come tomorrow

PRESENT PARTICIPLE

§ 47. *En* with the Present Participle always refers to the subject of the sentence.

(*a*) En forgeant on devient forgeron
By working at a forge one becomes a blacksmith

(*b*) Je l'ai vu en descendant l'escalier
I saw him as I came downstairs

(*c*) En arrivant à la gare il prit un taxi
On arriving at the station he took a taxi

(*d*) En essayant de monter il perdit pied
In *or* while trying to get in he lost his foothold

(*e*) Tout en parlant il agita les bras
As he spoke he waved his arms

(*f*) Rien qu'en tournant la manivelle vous le ferez marcher
Merely by turning the handle you will make it work

§ 48. Note.

Descendre	en	courant	Run downstairs
Entrer	,,	,,	Run in
Sortir	,,	,,	Run out
Traverser	,,	,,	Run across

Il s'approcha de moi en courant
He came running up to me

ENGLISH PRESENT PARTICIPLE

§ 49. After verbs of seeing and hearing the English Present Participle is translated by either the infinitive or a relative clause.

(*a*) Je le vis venir — I saw him coming

(*b*) Je l'entendis crier — I heard him shouting

(*c*) Je vis des hommes qui s'approchaient
I saw some men approaching

(*d*) J'entendis des enfants qui criaient
I heard some children shouting

§ 50. After *il y a* followed by a noun and also after *trouver* the English Present Participle is often translated by a relative clause.

Il y avait des gens **qui chantaient**	There were people **singing**
J'ai trouvé „ „ „ „	I found „ „

PAST PARTICIPLE

§ 51. The Past Participle agrees with the object, when the object precedes.

Voici la lettre, je l'ai écrite
La lettre que je vous ai écrite

POUVOIR, FALLOIR, DEVOIR, SAVOIR

§ 52. **Pouvoir.**

Je peux entrer? Est-ce que je peux entrer?	May I come in?
Il pourra pleuvoir demain	It may rain tomorrow
Pourriez-vous me dire...?	Could you tell me...?
Vous auriez pu insister	You could have (*or* might have) insisted

§ 53. **Falloir.**

(*a*) Il faut descendre	You must, we must get out
Faut-il y aller?	Must we / Have we to } go there?
(*b*) Il fallait descendre	We (*or* you) ought to have got out
Il fallait le dire	You should have said so
(*c*) Il faudra marcher plus vite	We shall have to walk quickly
(*d*) Il faudrait payer	You would have to pay

§ 54. **Devoir.**

(*a*) Il **doit** arriver demain	He **is to** arrive tomorrow
Vous **devez** être fatigué	You **must** be tired
Je **dois** aller chez le médecin	I **have to** go to the doctor's
(*b*) Il **devait** partir aujourd'hui	He **was to** start today

(*c*) Narrative.

Il **dut** changer de train — He **had to** change trains

(*d*) Il **a dû** se tromper d'heure — He **must have** mistaken the time

Conversational.

J'ai **dû** changer de train — I **had to** change trains

(*e*) Il **avait dû** changer d'habits — He **had had to** change his clothes

(*f*) 'Must have' in relation to another past event.

Il arriva en retard, il **avait dû** manquer le train
He arrived late, he **must have** missed the train

§ 55.

(*a*) Vous **devriez** lire Dickens — You **ought to** read Dickens

(*b*) Il **aurait dû** m'avertir — He **ought to have** warned me

§ 56. **Savoir.**

Je sais nager — I know how to swim
Je ne saurais vous le dire — I couldn't tell you

VERB + INFINITIVE WITHOUT PREPOSITION

§ 57. *Aimer* (also with *à* + inf.), like to, *compter*, expect to, *désirer*, want or desire to, *espérer*, hope to, *faillir* (to express 'nearly'), *oser*, dare to, *paraître*, appear to, *préférer*, prefer to, *sembler*, seem to, *vouloir*, be willing to, want to, *il vaut mieux*, it is better to, *avoir beau* + inf., do a thing in vain.

Il aime beaucoup jouer au football
He is very fond of playing football

Il espère vous voir — He hopes to see you
Il faillit tomber — He nearly fell
Je préfère y aller à pied — I prefer to walk there
Il vaut mieux se taire — It is better to be silent
Il eut beau protester — He protested in vain

Note. Cela vaut mieux que de faire du bruit
That is better than making a noise

§ 58.

(*a*) J'irai le voir	I will go **and** see him
(*b*) Il croyait rêver	He thought he was dreaming
Il croyait avoir trouvé	He thought he had found
Il crut entendre	He thought he heard
Je me rappelle l'avoir vu	I remember seeing him

§ 59. Ellipse of Infinitive.

Une auto qu'on disait très rapide (*être* omitted)
A car which was said to be very fast

§ 60. *FAIRE*

(*a*) Cela fit rire tout le monde
That made everyone laugh

Le froid lui fit trembler les mains
The cold made his hands shake

Il me fit asseoir He made me sit down

(*b*) When the infinitive after *faire* has an object, the object of *faire* (the person who is made to do something) is treated as indirect and is put into the dative.

J'ai fait étudier le français **à** mes élèves
I have made my pupils study French

The object of the infinitive after *faire* may be a noun clause.

Je **leur** ai fait voir **que**...
I have made them see that...

Cela **leur** fit croire que...
That made them believe that...

(*c*) Il le fit expédier	He had it despatched
Je l'ai fait réparer	I have had it repaired
(*d*) Il s'est fait couper les cheveux	He has had his hair cut

LAISSER

§ 61. Il laissa tomber sa canne	He dropped his stick
Il la laissa tomber	He dropped it
Laissez-moi parler	Let me speak

Se laisser guider par l'expérience
Let oneself be guided by experience

VOIR, ENTENDRE

§ 62. Je l'ai vu venir	I saw him come (*or* coming)
Il les entendit entrer	He heard them come in (*or* coming in)

SENTIR

§ 63. Je le sentis le prendre	I felt him take it

VERBS + *DE* + INFINITIVE

§ 64. (*a*) Transitive.

avertir quelqu'un de	warn someone to
empêcher quelqu'un de	prevent someone from (doing)
remercier quelqu'un de	thank someone for (doing)

(*b*) Intransitive.

craindre de	fear to, be afraid to	manquer de	fail to
daigner de	condescend to	oublier de	forget to
décider de	decide to	refuser de	refuse to
faire semblant de	pretend to	regretter de	be sorry to
finir de	finish (doing)	résoudre de	resolve to
se garder bien de	take care not to	se souvenir de	remember to

§ 65.

Je suis heureux de vous voir	I am happy to see you
Je suis content de vous voir	I am pleased (*or* glad) to see you
Je suis enchanté de vous voir	I am delighted to see you

Je regrette de ne pas savoir cela	I am sorry I don't know that I am afraid I don't know that
Je craignais J'avais peur } de ne pouvoir venir	I was afraid I should be unable to come

§ 66. Je le priai d'attendre	I begged him to wait
§ 67. Je ne pus m'empêcher de rire	I couldn't help laughing

§ 68. Il a eu la bonté de venir me voir
He has had the kindness to come and see me

Vous feriez mieux de vous en aller — You had better go away

§ 69.

(*a*) Il jugea préférable de	He thought it best to
Il trouva très étrange de	He thought it very strange to
Cela paraissait assez étrange de	It seemed rather strange to

(*b*) C'est très gentil **à** votre père **de** vous donner la permission
It is very kind **of** your father **to** give you leave

§ 70. Verbs taking dative of person followed by *de* with infinitive.

Le médecin a **commandé** au malade de rester au lit
The doctor has ordered the patient to remain in bed

Je lui ai **conseillé** de venir	I have advised him to come
„ „ **dit** „	„ told „ „
„ „ **demandé** „	„ asked „ „
„ „ **permis** „	„ allowed „ „
Dites-lui de se dépêcher	Tell him to hurry up
Son père lui **défendit** de sortir	His father forbade him to go out

§ 71. The above verbs cannot be used personally in the passive. Use either (*a*) *on* with an active verb

or (*b*) the impersonal passive.

(*a*) On lui a défendu de sortir — He has been forbidden to go out

(*b*) Il n'est pas permis aux voyageurs de traverser la voie
Passengers are not allowed to cross the line

§ 72. But *prier*, which takes a direct object, can be used personally in the passive.

On est prié de ne pas fumer — You are requested not to smoke

§ 73. The Historic Infinitive is only used in short sentences of the following type.

Et tout le monde **de rire**	And everybody laughed

À + INFINITIVE

§ 74. (*a*) Transitive verbs.

aider quelqu'un à	help someone to
inviter quelqu'un à	invite someone to

(*b*) Intransitive verbs.

apprendre à	learn to, learn how to		
commencer à se mettre à	begin to	continuer à	continue to
		réussir à	succeed in
consentir à	consent to	tenir à	be anxious to

§ 75.

Il demande à vous voir	He is asking to see you
Il ne tardera pas à venir	He won't be long in coming

§ 76. After phrases expressing duration of time and position.

(*a*)

Il passait son temps à travailler	He spent his time working
Il resta quelque temps à regarder	He remained some time looking
Elles sont toujours à bavarder	They are always (*or* still) chattering
Il était assis à lire...	He was sitting reading...

(*b*) *En train de* is a very common alternative after *assis* and similar verbs.

Il était assis en train de lire	He was sitting reading

§ 77.

J'ai beaucoup à faire	I have a great deal I have a lot } to do
Elle n'a rien à faire	She has nothing to do

J'ai un tas de choses à vous dire
I have a heap of things to tell you

Tout ce que vous avez à faire c'est de + infinitive
All you have to do is to...

Vous n'avez qu'à présenter votre billet
You have only to show your ticket

Quelque chose à manger	Something to eat
Il fut le premier à s'en aller	He was the first to go away

§ 78. The English passive is often used to translate sentences of the above type.

Il y a tant de choses à voir
There are so many things to be seen

Il y a du travail à faire
There is some work to be done

Il n'y a pas un instant à perdre
There is not a moment to be lost

§ 79. Il n'y a pas à dire	There is (*or* was) no mistake about it, certainly
§ 80. C'est à vous rendre fou	It is enough to make you mad

OTHER PREPOSITIONS + INFINITIVE

§ 81. (*a*) **Après avoir** déjeuné — After lunching

(Note that the perfect infinitive must be used after *après*.)

Avant de sortir	Before going out
Au lieu de répondre	Instead of replying
Loin d'en avoir peur	Far from being afraid of it (*or* them)
De peur de nous égarer	For fear of losing our way
Sans le savoir	Without knowing it

N.B. All the above must refer to the subject of the sentence.

e.g. Avant de partir je vous écrirai un mot

Before leaving / Before I leave } I will write you a line

(*b*) Il faut manger **pour** vivre
One must eat (in order) to live

Faire un effort **pour**...	Make an effort to...
Faire son possible / Faire de son mieux } **pour**...	Do one's best to...

Il fait assez chaud **pour** se baigner
It is warm enough to bathe

Il est trop jeune **pour** savoir He is too young to know

(*c*) Il fut puni **pour avoir** transgressé la loi
He was punished for having broken the law

(*d*) Il alla **jusqu'à** m'insulter
He went so far as to insult me

(*e*) Il commença **par** refuser He began by refusing
Il finit **par** accepter He ended by accepting

INFINITIVE + INTERROGATIVE OR RELATIVE

§ 82. Que faire? { What am I to do? / What are we to do? }

Je ne sais que faire I don't know what to do
Pourquoi faire tant de façons? Why make so much fuss?

Je ne sais pas comment vous remercier
I don't know how to thank you

Je ne trouve pas de quoi écrire
I can't find anything to write with

SUBJUNCTIVE

§ 83. Sequence of Tenses.

PRIMARY. { Present Indicative / Future Indicative / Perfect Indicative } + { Present Subjunctive / Perfect Subjunctive }

HISTORIC. { Imperfect Indicative / Past Definite Indicative / Pluperfect Indicative } + { Imperfect Subjunctive / Pluperfect Subjunctive }

Note. (*a*) The Present Subjunctive is used to represent future time.

Je crains qu'il ne soit en retard
I am afraid he will be late

(*b*) When a Primary tense is required to represent past time, use the Perfect Subjunctive.

Je suis content que vous ayez pu venir
I am glad you were able to come

SUBJUNCTIVE AFTER VERBS

§ 84. Je veux que vous veniez — I want you to come
Je voulais qu'il le fît — I wanted him to do it
Voulez-vous que nous sortions? — Shall we go out?
Où voulez-vous que je le mette? — Where shall I put it?

À quelle heure voulez-vous qu'il vienne?
What time do you want him to come?

Que voulez-vous que j'y fasse?
What do you expect me to do about it?

Je voudrais qu'il parlât. — I wish he would speak

§ 85. Je suis content / „ enchanté } que vous puissiez venir

I am glad / „ delighted } that you can come

Je suis content que vous ayez pu venir
I am glad you were able to come

Elle fut enchantée qu'il fût venu
She was delighted he had come

Je regrette qu'il soit absent — I am sorry he is away

Je regrette que vous n'ayez pas pu venir
I am sorry you were unable to come

§ 86. Je crains qu'il (ne) vous voie
I am afraid he may (*or* will) see you

Je craignais qu'il (ne) tombât — I was afraid he would fall
Je crains qu'il ne vous voie pas — I am afraid he will not see you

§ 87. Il ordonna qu'on amenât le prisonnier
He ordered the prisoner to be brought

Il supplia qu'on lui permît de venir
He begged to be allowed to come

§ 88. Attendez qu'il vienne — Wait till he comes

J'attendais qu'il arrivât — I was waiting for him to arrive

Il attendait qu'on lui apportât l'addition
He was waiting for the bill to be brought

§ 89. Je tiens absolument à ce qu'il vienne
I insist on his coming

Je tenais absolument à ce qu'il le fît
I was determined that he should do so

SUBJUNCTIVE AFTER CONJUNCTIONS

§ 90. (*a*) Parlez plus haut, **pour qu**'on vous entende mieux
Speak louder, so that they may hear you better

Il est assez tard **pour qu**'il ait fini son travail
It is late enough for him to have finished his work

Il n'y a pas de chance **pour que** cela arrive
There's no chance of that happening

(*b*) **Bien qu**'il / **Quoiqu**'il } soit pauvre, il est généreux
Though he is poor, he is generous

(*c*) *Bien que* and *quoique* can be used with an adjective or participle, when the subject of the main and dependent clauses is the same.

Quoique fâché, il ne dit rien
Although he was vexed, he said nothing

(*d*) Il ne fera rien **à moins que** vous **ne** l'ordonniez
He will do nothing unless you order it

(*e*) **Avant que** vous partiez, je vous écrirai un mot
Before you leave, I will write you a line

Il y resta **jusqu'à ce qu**'on vînt le chercher
He remained there till they came to fetch him

(*f*) Faites tout ce que vous voudrez, **pourvu que** vous me laissiez tranquille
Do what you like, provided (*or* so long as) you leave me alone

Pourvu qu'il vienne ! — I only hope he will come !

(*g*) **Qu'il soit maître ou valet**
Whether he is a master or a servant

IMPERSONAL EXPRESSIONS + SUBJUNCTIVE

§ 91. Il faut que vous y alliez — You must go there
Faudra-t-il que nous y allions? — Shall we have to go there?

Il est possible que vous ayez raison
It is possible that you are (*or* may be) right

Il est honteux qu'on dise cela
It is shameful that they should say that

§ 92. Nul doute qu'il y ait foule
No doubt there will be a crowd

SUBJUNCTIVE IN RELATIVE CLAUSES

§ 93. Relative clauses depending on a superlative, *seul*, *premier* or *dernier*, in the main clause.

C'est **la seule** chose que je puisse vous offrir
It is the only thing that I can offer you

C'était **le plus beau** livre qu'il eût jamais lu
It was the finest book he had ever read.

§ 94. Relative clauses dependent on a negative or indefinite word or expression in the main clause.

Il **ne** trouva **personne** qui voulût l'aider
He found no one who was willing to help him

Il me demanda si j'avais vu **quelque** petite maison qui me plût
He asked me if I had seen any little house which I liked

PREPOSITIONS

§ 95. **à.**

(*a*) À dix milles de Londres — Ten miles from London
À quelques pas de la maison — A few steps from the house

(*b*) Il le tenait à la main — He was holding it in his hand

(*c*) Une femme aux cheveux noirs — A woman with black hair

§ 96. chez.

Il rentra chez lui	He returned home
Il arriva chez lui	He arrived home
Il passa chez le boucher	He called at the butcher's

§ 97. de.

(*a*) Parler d'un ton doux — Speak in a gentle tone
„ d'une voix claire — „ „ clear voice

(*b*) Je ne l'ai jamais vu de toute ma vie
I have never seen him in all my life

Je n'ai pas dormi de toute la nuit
I have not slept all night

(*c*)	Le meilleur élève de la classe	The best boy in the class
(*d*)	Plus de dix francs	More than ten francs
(*e*)	Il a neuf cents pieds de haut	It is nine hundred feet high
(*f*)	Mourir de faim	Die of hunger
	Trembler de froid	Shake with cold
(*g*)	Entouré d'arbres	Surrounded with trees
	Frappé d'étonnement	Struck with astonishment
	Saisi d'horreur	Seized with horror
	„ de peur	„ „ fear

§ 98. d'entre.

Quelqu'un d'entre vous	Any of you
Quelques-uns d'entre nous	Some of us

§ 99. en.

(*a*) **en** été, **en** automne, **en** hiver, but **au** printemps.

(*b*) To express time within which.

On peut aller à Londres en trois heures

(*Dans* expresses 'time after which', e.g. Je partirai dans une heure.)

§ 100. par.

(*a*) Par une belle matinée de printemps
On a beautiful spring morning

Par une belle nuit de Provence	On a lovely night in Provence
Par un jour d'hiver	On a winter's day
Par temps de brouillard	In foggy weather

(*b*) Passer la tête par la fenêtre
Put one's head out of the window

Regarder par la fenêtre — Look out of the window
Jeter par la fenêtre — Throw out of the window

(*c*) Trois fois par semaine — Three times a week

§ 101. pendant, 'for', 'during' (of past time).

Pendant quelque temps — For some time

§ 102. pour, 'for' (of future time).

Pour combien de temps êtes-vous ici?
For how long are you here?

§ 103. sur.

(*a*) Prendre la clef sur la table — Take the key off the table

(*b*) Répondre sur un ton de reproche
Reply in a tone of reproach

§ 104. Sauter **à bas de** son lit — Jump out of one's bed

ADVERBS

§ 105. aussitôt.

Aussitôt dit, aussitôt fait — No sooner said than done

§ 106. combien.

Je ne saurais vous dire combien je vous suis reconnaissant
I cannot tell you how grateful I am to you

§ 107. comme, 'how!' exclamatory.

Comme il fait chaud! — How hot it is!

Comme vous devez être fatigué!
How tired you must be!

Vous ne savez pas comme il est amusant!
You don't know how amusing he is!

Note that the order of the words is the same as in an affirmative sentence, and not the inverted order as in English.

§ 108. que is often used in the same sense as *comme.*

Que c'est vrai !	How true it is !
Que j'étais heureux !	How happy I was !

Que vous avez de belles mains !
What beautiful hands you have !

§ 109. plus.

Aller de plus en plus vite	Go faster and faster

Plus je lis de livres, plus j'apprends
The more books I read, the more I learn

SOME ENGLISH WORDS

§ 110. happen.

Qu'est-ce qui vous / „ „ lui } est arrivé?	What has happened to you? / „ „ him?

§ 111. late.

(*a*) Of people.

Être en retard	Be late
Être en retard de cinq minutes	Be five minutes late
Arriver dix minutes en retard / Arriver avec un retard de dix minutes	Arrive ten minutes late

(*b*) Of trains.

Avoir du retard	Be late
Avoir dix minutes de retard	Be ten minutes late
Avoir autant de retard que...	Be as late as...

§ 112. matter.

Qu'est-ce qu'il y a? / Qu'y a-t-il?	What is the matter?
Je ne sais pas ce qu'il y a	I don't know what is the matter

Il se demanda ce qu'il pouvait bien y avoir
He wondered what could be the matter

Qu'est-ce que cela fait?	What does it matter?
Cela ne fait rien	It doesn't matter
N'importe	No matter

§ 113. people.

(*a*) Beaucoup de monde — Many people
Tant de monde — So many people

(*b*) Les gens chics — Smart people
Ces gens là-haut — Those people up there
Les gens d'ici — People here

§ 114. take.

(*a*) (a thing to a place): porter

(*b*) (a person to a place): conduire, amener

§ 115. stand.

(*a*) (of people): se tenir (debout)

(*b*) (of things): se trouver, être situé

§ 116. year.

(*a*) With cardinal numbers *l'an.*

e.g. Deux ans — Two years

(*b*) With ordinal numbers, adjectives, and adjectival pronouns, *l'année.*

e.g. La deuxième année — The second year
L'année dernière — Last year
Quelques années — Some *or* a few years

SOME FRENCH WORDS

§ 117. s'asseoir.

Je m'assieds — I sit down
Il s'assit — He sat down
Je suis assis — I am sitting
Il était assis — He was sitting

§ 118. depuis.

(*a*) Preposition.

Je ne l'ai pas vu depuis quelques années
I have not seen him for some years

(*b*) Adverb.

Je ne l'ai pas vu depuis	I have not seen him since

§ 119. devenir.

Qu'est devenu votre frère? Qu'est-ce que votre frère est devenu?	What has become of your brother?
Qu'est-il devenu? Qu'est-ce qu'il est devenu?	What has become of him?

Je ne sais pas ce que votre frère est devenu
I don't know what has become of your brother

Je ne sais pas ce qu'il est devenu
I don't know what has become of him

§ 120. manquer.

Vous nous manquez beaucoup	We miss you very much
Votre père doit vous manquer	You must miss your father

IRREGULAR VERBS

Infinitive	Participles	Present Indicative
aller *to go*	allant, allé	je vais, tu vas, il va, nous allons, ils vont
s'asseoir *to sit*	s'asseyant assis	je m'assieds, il s'assied, nous nous asseyons, ils s'asseyent
battre *to beat*	battant battu	je bats, il bat, nous battons, ils battent
boire *to drink*	buvant, bu	je bois, il boit, nous buvons, ils boivent
conduire *to lead*	conduisant conduit	je conduis, il conduit, nous conduisons, ils conduisent
connaître *to be acquainted with*	connaissant connu	je connais, il connaît, nous connaissons, ils connaissent
coudre *to sew*	cousant cousu	je couds, il coud, nous cousons, ils cousent
courir *to run*	courant couru	je cours, il court, nous courons, ils courent
craindre *to fear*	craignant craint	je crains, il craint, nous craignons, ils craignent
croire *to believe*	croyant, cru	je crois, il croit, nous croyons, ils croient
devoir *to owe*	devant, dû Note fem. *due*	je dois, il doit, nous devons, ils doivent
dire *to say*	disant, dit	je dis, il dit, nous disons, vous dites, ils disent
écrire *to write*	écrivant écrit	j'écris, il écrit, nous écrivons, ils écrivent
envoyer *to send*	envoyant envoyé	j'envoie, nous envoyons, ils envoient
faire *to make*	faisant, fait	je fais, il fait, nous faisons, vous faites, ils font
lire *to read*	lisant, lu	je lis, il lit, nous lisons, ils lisent
mettre *to put*	mettant, mis	je mets, il met, nous mettons, ils mettent
mourir *to die*	mourant mort	je meurs, il meurt, nous mourons, ils meurent

Past Definite Passé Historique	Future	Present Subjunctive and Notes
j'allai	j'irai	que j'aille, nous allions, ils aillent. Imperative: *va*, *allons*, *allez*
je m'assis	je m'assiérai	„ je m'asseye, etc.
je battis	je battrai	„ je batte, etc.
je bus	je boirai	„ je boive, nous buvions, ils boivent
je conduisis	je conduirai	„ je conduise, etc.
je connus	je connaîtrai	„ je connaisse, etc. N.B. Always *î* circumflex before *t*
je cousis	je coudrai	„ je couse, etc.
je courus	je courrai	„ je coure, etc.
je craignis	je craindrai	„ je craigne, etc. Verbs in *-aindre*, *-eindre* and *-oindre* are conjugated like *craindre*, e.g. *plaindre*, *feindre*, *atteindre*, *joindre*
je crus	je croirai	„ je croie, etc.
je dus	je devrai	„ je doive, nous devions, ils doivent
je dis	je dirai	„ je dise, etc.
j'écrivis	j'écrirai	„ j'écrive, etc.
j'envoyai	j'enverrai	„ j'envoie, etc.
je fis	je ferai	„ je fasse, etc.
je lus	je lirai	„ je lise, etc.
je mis	je mettrai	„ je mette, etc.
je mourus	je mourrai	„ je meure, nous mourions, ils meurent. N.B. Compound tenses with *être*

Infinitive	Participles	Present Indicative
naître *to be born*	naissant, né	je nais, il naît, nous naissons, ils naissent
pleuvoir *to rain*	pleuvant plu	il pleut
pouvoir *to be able*	pouvant, pu	je peux *or* je puis, tu peux, il peut, nous pouvons, ils peuvent
prendre *to take*	prenant pris	je prends, il prend, nous prenons, ils prennent
résoudre *to resolve*	résolvant résolu	je résous, il résout, nous résolvons, ils résolvent
rire *to laugh*	riant, ri	je ris, il rit, nous rions, ils rient
rompre *to break*	rompant rompu	je romps, il rompt, nous rompons, etc.
savoir *to know (a fact)*	sachant, su	je sais, nous savons, ils savent
suivre *to follow*	suivant suivi	je suis, il suit, nous suivons, ils suivent
se taire *to be silent*	se taisant, tu	je me tais, nous nous taisons, ils se taisent
tenir *to hold*	tenant, tenu	je tiens, il tient, nous tenons, ils tiennent
vaincre *to conquer*	vainquant vaincu	je vaincs, il vainc, nous vainquons, ils vainquent
valoir *to be worth*	valant, valu	je vaux, il vaut, nous valons, ils valent
venir *to come*	venant venu	je viens, il vient, nous venons, ils viennent
vêtir *to clothe*	vêtant vêtu	je vêts, il vêt, nous vêtons, ils vêtent
vivre *to live*	vivant vécu	je vis, il vit, nous vivons, ils vivent
voir *to see*	voyant, vu	je vois, il voit, nous voyons, ils voient
vouloir *to wish*	voulant voulu	je veux, il veut, nous voulons, ils veulent

Past Definite Passé Historique	Future	Present Subjunctive and Notes
je naquis	je naîtrai	que je naisse, etc. N.B. Compound tenses with *être*. Note *î* before *t*
il plut	il pleuvra	qu'il pleuve, etc.
je pus	je pourrai	que je puisse, etc.
je pris	je prendrai	„ je prenne, etc.
je résolus	je résoudrai	„ je résolve, etc.
je ris	je rirai	„ je rie, etc.
je rompis	je romprai	„ je rompe, etc.
je sus	je saurai	„ je sache, etc. Imperative: *sache, sachons, sachez*
je suivis	je suivrai	„ je suive, etc.
je me tus	je me tairai	„ je me taise, etc.
je tins	je tiendrai	„ je tienne, nous tenions, ils tiennent. 3rd sing. imperf. subj. *tînt*
je vainquis	je vaincrai	„ je vainque, etc.
je valus	je vaudrai	„ je vaille, nous valions, ils vaillent
*je vins	je viendrai	„ je vienne, nous venions, ils viennent. 3rd sing. imperf. subj. *vînt*
je vêtis	je vêtirai	„ je vête, etc.
je vécus	je vivrai	„ je vive, etc.
je vis	je verrai	„ je voie, etc.
je voulus	je voudrai	„ je veuille, nous voulions, ils veuillent. Note the imperative *veuillez*, 'be so good as to'

* Je vins, tu vins, il vint, nous vînmes, vous vîntes, ils vinrent.

Section II

PASSAGES FOR FRENCH PROSE

A. *EXAMINATION PAPERS*

I

The other day, as I was walking along[1] the street, a gentleman came up to me and called me by my name. 'Excuse me, Sir,' I said to him, 'but are you not mistaken?'[2] 'You do not remember[3] me, then? We used to[4] meet each other very often in London.' 'Really![5] my old friend Brown! I remember you now, and I am glad to see you again. Is your wife here too?'[6] 'No, unfortunately, she is not;[7] I am here for a few days, and I was hoping to find you.' 'What a pleasure![8] come and[9] see me at my house this evening, will you?'[10] 'Yes, I shall come with pleasure.'[11] I gave him my address and he left me, but I have not seen him since.[12]

(Cambridge Local Junior, December 1930)

1 *se promener dans.* 2 be mistaken, *se tromper*, or *faire erreur.* 3 Translate 'remember' by *remettre.* 4 § 38. 5 *Tiens!* 6 'Your wife is here, she too?' 7 'Unfortunately not' (*pas*). 8 § 10 (*b*). 9 § 58 (*a*). 10 *voulez-vous?* 11 *très volontiers* (to avoid repetition of *plaisir*). 12 Say 'I have not seen him again (*revoir*).'

II

One winter evening a gentleman entered an inn; there were so many people[1] in the room[2] that it was impossible to get[3] a seat near the fire. He looked round him[4] for a moment, then turned to the waiter and said, 'Waiter, take a dozen oysters to my horse which is in the stable.' The waiter looked astonished, but went out with[5] the oysters. The people[6] who were in the room rose and followed him to see this strange animal that ate oysters. They returned in a few minutes and found the gentleman sitting comfortably[7] near the fire. 'Sir,' said the waiter, 'your horse will not[8] eat the oysters.' 'Well, in that case,'[9] was the reply, 'bring them here and I shall eat them myself.'

oyster, *une huître*

(Cambridge Local Junior, July 1931)

1 § 3 (*d*). 2 *la salle*. 3 *trouver*. 4 § 9 (*a*). 5 Translate 'with' by *en emportant*. 6 *les gens*. 7 *confortablement installé*. 8 'is not willing.' 9 *en ce cas-là*.

III

A young servant had been sent[1] to the town with a ring.[2] As he was crossing a bridge he took the ring out of its box to look at it and let it fall into the water. He searched for it for[3] several hours but he was not able to find it. Fearing to return to[4] his master, he ran away. He went to America and became very rich. After many years,[5] he came back to England and bought the house of his former master. One day, while he was walking[6] on the bridge with a friend, he told him the story of the ring. 'This is[7] the place', he said, and put the end of his stick into a hole of an old tree. When he had drawn out the stick he was very surprised to see the ring.

(Cambridge Local Junior, December 1932)

1 Avoid passive by using *on*, § 17 (*b*). 2 'to take a ring to the town.' 3 What preposition? 4 *rentrer chez*. 5 § 3 (*a*). 6 *se promener*. 7 *Voici*.

IV

One day during the summer when[1] it was very hot, the boys who had finished their lessons at one o'clock, set out with Don, our faithful dog, to pass the afternoon in the field near the river. They played for[2] a long time, then they sat down under some trees to read their books. Suddenly they heard a cry, they raised their[3] eyes and they saw a little girl in the river. Don, who had been sleeping[4] until that moment, threw himself into the water and seized the dress of the child. The boys followed their dog and helped him to[5] save her.

(Cambridge Local Junior, December 1933)

1 when, *alors que*. 2 Omit 'for'. 3 § 1 (*h*). 4 Imperfect. 5 *aider*, § 74 (*a*).

V

From France to England by Aeroplane

Use the Perfect, not the Past Definite.

Far beneath us we saw long straight[1] roads, yellow fields, very few houses, several churches and at last the blue sea. We followed the coast for a few minutes and then there was only[2] water. We were crossing the Channel. We passed over a steamer which resembled the boat that my brother gave me last Christmas. Shortly afterwards we were looking at England out of[3] the window. England is very like France, but there are hedges round the fields, and the roads are not so straight. All at once I perceived that the aeroplane was coming down, and then I saw that it was running along the grass. We had arrived at Croydon.

(Cambridge Local Junior, July 1934)

1 § 4 (*c*). 2 § 3 (*c*). 3 *par*.

VI

One day, an old lady who had a parrot left the door of his cage open.[1] He flew[2] immediately into a wood that was near the house and began to talk to the birds which he saw there. In the evening,[3] when the sun was setting, a young peasant passed carrying a gun. The poor parrot, seized with fear, exclaimed, 'Good day, sir!' The young man, astonished, let his gun fall[4] and said, 'Excuse me, sir, I thought you were a bird.' The parrot, without saying anything,[5] set off for the house, where he was happy to[6] find that the old lady was waiting for him.

(Cambridge Local Junior, December 1935)

1 'left open the door of his cage.' 2 *s'envoler*. 3 § 1 (*b*). 4 § 61. 5 § 6 (*d*). 6 § 65.

VII

Use 2nd Person Singular throughout.

My dear Father,

Do you remember a letter I wrote you several months ago? I had just arrived in England. How unhappy I was![1] I wanted to return home at once. When I told my grandparents so,[2] they smiled. 'We will see tomorrow,' they replied, 'you are tired now.'

They were right. The next morning I had forgotten all my troubles. As I have told you more than[3] once, I have enjoyed myself very much[4] here and learned many things.[5] Of course, now[6] the moment has come, I am not sorry to leave. Be at the station and tell Henri to[7] be there too....

(Northern Universities Matriculation, September 1931)

1 For order of words see § 108. 2 For 'so' say 'it'. 3 § 97 (*d*). 4 very much, *bien*. 5 § 3 (*a*). 6 *maintenant que*. 7 For construction see § 70.

VIII

She was sitting by her bedroom fire,[1] reading[2] a book about the French revolution. It was such an[3] interesting story that she quite[4] forgot the time. She was much[5] astonished, therefore, when a clock struck midnight.[6] 'I ought to have been in bed an hour ago', she said to herself.

She was going to put out the light when she heard someone coming[7] upstairs. She was not a brave woman and she was alone in the house. The footsteps grew more and more distinct. She didn't know what to do.[8] If she had shouted for help who would have heard her?

(Northern Universities Matriculation, July 1931)

1 'in her bedroom by (*auprès de*) the fire.' 2 *en train de*+inf. 3 § 17 (*d*). 4 *complètement*. 5 much, *très*. 6 'when midnight struck by (*à*) the clock.' 7 § 49 (*b*). 8 § 82.

IX

Use the Past Definite for the past tenses, not the Perfect.

Madame du Deffand was once asked:[1] 'Do you believe in ghosts?' 'No, but I'm afraid of them',[2] she replied. Without confessing it many people[3] resemble Madame du Deffand. Several years ago my brother and one or two friends of his[4] were invited to spend a few days with[5] a lady living in an old sixteenth-century house.

On[6] the evening of their arrival someone told a ghost story. After[7] he had finished everyone laughed[8] saying there are no ghosts nowadays.[9] The braver spirits added they would like to meet one.[10] 'I am so glad to hear you say that', murmured the hostess. 'I was wondering to whom I could give the haunted bedroom.'

ghost, *revenant*, m. to haunt, *hanter*

(Northern Universities Matriculation, September 1932)

1 § 23. 2 § 8 (*b*). 3 § 3 (*a*). 4 'one or two of his friends.' 5 *chez*. 6 § 1 (*b*). 7 *lorsque*+2nd pluperf., § 44. 8 *se mettre à rire*. 9 § 6 (*a*). 10 § 8 (*b*).

X

My sister will be fifteen years old on the twentieth of June and she has been[1] in London for nearly five years.

Before coming to work in London she used to live in the South of England and she has been to Paris several times with my uncle and me.

When we were in Paris we all used to go for a walk or a drive[2] in the Bois de Boulogne every morning before half-past eleven.

Then, after lunching[3] at our hotel, my uncle would[4] go up to his room to busy himself with his letters,[5] but my sister and I usually visited the principal shops, unless it were[6] too hot.

(Northern Universities Matriculation, July 1934)

1 § 37 (*a*). 2 *faire une promenade à pied ou en auto.* 3 § 81 (*a*). 4 § 38 (*c*). 5 his letters, *son courrier.* 6 § 90 (*d*).

XI

When I am[1] rich I shall build a little house in the country, perhaps on a hill surrounded with trees, and fairly near the sea. I do not like the life of large towns especially in spring and in summer. It is always too hot in their streets and work is very tiring.

In the country I should be able to go for long walks every day, and if I lived at the seaside I should soon learn to swim. However, I prefer to live in town during the first two[2] months of the year, for it is less cold there and there are many interesting things to[3] see.

(Northern Universities Matriculation, September 1934)

1 § 39. 2 'the two first.' 3 § 77.

XII

When you come[1] to see me in the country we shall go for long walks on the hills and in the woods.

Do not forget to bring your gun, for I know you are fond of hunting and my uncle will be delighted to go with you.

I am glad you are[2] coming in spring, for in summer it is very hot here and we have too many people in the village.

I shall be able to meet[3] you at the station with father, and if you are not too tired we shall walk back and ask father to[4] bring your luggage to the farm in the car.

(Northern Universities Matriculation, July 1935)

1 Tense? 2 § 85. 3 meet, *attendre*. 4 § 70.

XIII

(*a*) I was taking a walk in the country the other day when I met an old school friend.[1] (*b*) We had not seen each other for more than twenty years.[2] (*c*) We were well pleased to meet, and chatted for a long time. (*d*) We had many things to[3] tell each other. (*e*) He told me, among other things, that his eldest son was now a pupil at our old school.[4] (*f*) I found he was living at Tedfold, only four miles from[5] here. (*g*) As I had nothing to[6] do, I accompanied him as far as his home, where he introduced me to his wife and children. (*h*) He is a doctor, and has just settled (*s'établir*) in this district. (*i*) He invited us to pay him a visit next Friday. (*j*) Of course, we shall go,[7] if the weather is fine.

(Matriculation, June 1928)

1 *un ancien camarade de collège*. 2 § 7 (*b*) or § 118 (*a*). 3 § 77.
4 *notre ancien collège*. 5 § 95 (*a*). 6 § 77. 7 'we shall go there.'

XIV

1. I have been learning French for[1] several years, and every summer I go to France. 2. Last year we spent our holidays on the coast of Brittany. 3. Instead of going[2] to a big hotel, like most travellers, we found lodgings[3] in a small cottage.[4] 4. The cottage was quite near the harbour, and it belonged to one of the fishermen. 5. The latter had a boat of his own,[5] and he would[6] fish all day long, and sometimes all night. 6. His wife did all the housework, and also cultivated a large garden. 7. One evening her husband invited us to accompany him, and we spent the whole night at sea. 8. It was four o'clock in[7] the morning when we returned to the little port. 9. Unfortunately the weather was not very fine; during the first week it rained nearly every day. 10. If it had been fine, we should have stayed there till the end of September.

(Matriculation, September 1928)

1 § 37 (*a*). 2 *descendre dans.* 3 *trouver à nous loger.* 4 *une petite maison.* 5 *un bateau à lui.* 6 Tense? 7 What preposition in French?

XV

1. Do you remember my cousin Jack? Yes, what has become of him?[1] 2. When I saw him for the last time, five years ago, he had just left school. 3. He was very fond of the country, and told me he was going to be a[2] farmer. 4. Everybody told him that he would never make his fortune in that way. 5. At last he followed his parents' advice, and became a bank clerk (*employé de banque*). 6. But one evening, he looked very unhappy; instead of eating his supper, he went for a long walk. 7. When he came back he told his father he would never be happy as a[3] clerk in London. 8. Well, my boy, his father said to him, perhaps[4] you are right after all. 9. Here is a letter from my cousin that I have received this morning. 10. He has been

in Australia for the last six months,[5] and is much happier than he was[6] in London.

(Matriculation, January 1930)

1 § 119. 2 § 2 (*a*). 3 § 2 (*b*). 4 § 32. 5 § 37 (*a*). 6 § 7 (*a*).

XVI

1. I have just received your charming letter; it has given (*faire*) me great pleasure. 2. I shall be pleased to go and see you. I will arrive next Tuesday by the ten o'clock train. 3. I am glad you have[1] not forgotten the happy days we have spent together. 4. I saw you for the last time three years ago. 5. Last month my mother was very ill, but she is better now. 6. How is George? He is twenty-one now, isn't he?[2] 7. I have not forgotten your beautiful house and the pleasant walks which we had (*faire*) together. 8. Do you remember the excursion which we made one day to an old church? 9. I should like to visit it again if we have time. 10. I will tell you all the news when I arrive.[3]

(Matriculation, June 1930)

1 § 85. 2 *n'est-ce pas?* 3 Tense?

XVII

1. We are very pleased to hear[1] that you are coming to France this year. 2. My husband has known for[2] years the hotel which you speak of. 3. Two years ago we spent the summer holidays there. 4. The hotel is quite near the sea, and only a few hundred[3] metres from the station. 5. The proprietor is a most intelligent man, and speaks English very well. 6. I am sure he has not forgotten us. 7. Ask him if he remembers Monsieur and Madame Dupont, and their children. 8. Before returning to England you must[4] come and see us. 9. As you will see by[5] our address, we are no longer in Paris. 10. We have bought a pretty little house in the country, about ten[6] kilometres from Étampes.

(Matriculation, September 1930)

1 *savoir*. 2 § 37 (*a*). 3 *quelques centaines de*. 4 § 91.
5 Preposition? 6 about ten, *une dizaine de*.

XVIII

(*a*) There is little news. Charlotte has gone to Deauville, where she will stay a fortnight. (*b*) When you see her, give her Jeanne's address. (*c*) André, the friend we were expecting tomorrow, is too ill to[1] come. (*d*) He has just written to me that the doctor has forbidden him to come. (*e*) He needs a long rest. I hope they (*on*) will send him into the country. (*f*) Charlotte was hoping he would keep us company till her return. (*g*) Could you send me a few books? We spend all our time here in[2] reading. (*h*) We play tennis occasionally, but we know so few people. (*i*) If only it kept fine! The only time the sun has shown itself, we were asleep! (*j*) I am sorry this letter is[3] not more interesting, but nothing happens in our village.

(Matriculation, January 1931)

1 § 81 (*b*) p. 22. 2 § 76 (*a*). 3 Mood?

XIX

1. After reading several pages, Joan, sitting under an old tree, fell asleep. 2. It was so pleasant[1] out of doors that she did not wake up until half-past four. 3. After tea she took her bicycle and went along a pretty road. 4. On arriving at Peter's house she left her machine near the garden gate. 5. Peter soon appeared from[2] a corner of the garden and was delighted that she had come. 6. 'When I have filled my basket with cherries,' he said, 'I will come for a walk.' 7. 'Very well,' Joan replied, 'and we will buy some eggs at the farm, although they are dear. 8. And let me help you; I will hold the basket. Give me it.' 9. The cherries which he had already gathered* were big and white. 10. 'Let us not eat too many,' cried Peter, 'or we shall not want to go for the eggs.'

* Use *cueillir*.

(Matriculation, June 1931)

1 it is pleasant, *il fait bon*. 2 Say 'coming from'. The word *apparaître* cannot by itself express 'motion from'.

XX

(1) *A.*—I believe Roberts has come back. I'll go and see. (2) *A.*—Yes, there he is. I shall ask him to fetch your baggage. (3) *B.*—Thanks, but he won't be able to carry it. Tell him to take a taxi. (4) *A.*—Very well. Now let us take tea and talk. I have a lot to tell you. (5) *B.*—You are very kind, but I ought not to stay, you know. (6) *A.*—Perhaps. But I am glad you are here. Do sit down.[1] (7) *B.*—I am really very tired. It is a fatiguing journey. Have you ever been to Bude? (8) *A.*—Yes, a few years ago, after a long illness. My brothers often go there. (9) *B.*—I should like to spend the whole summer there. And you? (10) *A.*—I? No. I should prefer to travel in Germany and Switzerland, as I do now.[2]

(Matriculation, June 1932)

1 'Sit down, I beg you (*je vous en prie*).' 2 'as I do it now.'

XXI

1. We will not go to the seaside next Saturday, as[1] it may[2] rain. 2. There are so many other ways of spending a pleasant day. 3. Before breakfast we will swim in the lake at the end of the park. 4. About ten o'clock we ought to hear something good on[3] the wireless. 5. Then let us go for a walk in the woods where all the birds are singing. 6. In the afternoon we must meet a few friends whom I have invited. 7. If they come we will go on the river and take tea. 8. The countryside is already pretty; the meadows are full of flowers. 9. At sunset we hope to see a pretty sky behind that hill. 10. And later, it is possible we may hear[4] the nightingale.

(Matriculation, September 1932)

1 *car*. 2 What tense of *pouvoir*? 3 *par*. 4 § 91.

XXII

1. They tell me you have just come back from France. Are you better? 2. Yes, but I am rather tired. We arrived two hours late[1] on account of a storm. 3. Most of my companions were afraid, although there was no danger. 4. In such a case[2] one always wonders what is going to happen. 5. I was thinking chiefly of the friends who were waiting for me, for it was so cold. 6. Did you succeed in seeing all the places you wished to visit in France? 7. I had to abandon the idea of going to Avignon because I had no more money. 8. What a pity! The Popes' Palace and the picturesque old bridge are well worth[3] a visit. 9. Several Frenchmen have told me so,[4] and I hope to be able to go there next year. 10. No part[5] of the country pleased me more.[6] Try not to miss it.

(Matriculation, June 1933)

1 § 111 (*a*). 2 *Dans un cas pareil.* 3 *valoir bien.* 4 'have told me it.' 5 *la région.* 6 *davantage.*

XXIII

1. If you will[1] come and see me we can talk about that matter. 2. Let us hope it will not rain; then we shall be able to go into the country. 3. We will smoke, you your pipe, and I cigarettes. That helps conversation, and I have much to tell you. 4. It is possible that one of my friends will arrive[2] a little later in the afternoon. 5. I am afraid he will be[3] tired. We ought not to make him talk much. 6. I am glad he is coming, for he is a most interesting man[4] and has travelled a great deal. 7. He has written several books in which he describes his adventures in foreign countries. 8. He and his wife spent a few days with us some months ago, but we have not seen them since. 9. Those who do not know her well sometimes think she is rather vain. 10. They are wrong, however; in fact no one is more modest than she.

(Matriculation, September 1933)

1 § 46. 2 Mood? 3 Mood? 4 § 4 (*d*).

XXIV

1. Let us cross the road and go into that bookshop, where we shall be able to find what you want. 2. The old man who is the owner of it has lived there for more than thirty years. 3. His only son, of whom he was very fond, went to America when he was sixteen. 4. No one knows whether he is still alive, but his father thinks he will never see him again. 5. They say the old man is nearly blind, yet he never complains and is always good-tempered. 6. I am afraid he will never be rich, for he is more interested in books than in money. 7. While his sight was good, he was never happier than when reading.[1] He spent much time in that way. 8. That has now become impossible, but he still loves his books as much as before.[2] 9. When he learns that you are a student, he will do all that he can to[3] help you. 10. If you ask him, he will no doubt lend you one or two novels for the holidays.

(Matriculation, January 1934)

1 'when he was reading.' 2 before, *par le passé*. 3 § 81 (*b*).

XXV

1. Isn't it cold this evening? Let us sit in front of the fire. 2. Put some coal on the flames. We will dream as[1] we look at the smoke. 3. Which of the armchairs will you take, this or that? I like the red one.[2] 4. Although we can hear the north wind outside, we are comfortable here. 5. The lamp is lit; now draw the curtains; soon we shall be having wine and biscuits. 6. Perhaps you prefer hot coffee. In that case, kindly ring the bell. 7. Do not forget that tomorrow is Friday,[3] a busy day for us both. 8. Yes, that is why[4] we must go to bed not later than eleven o'clock. 9. There is a lot of work to be done[5] at my office, so I ought to get there early. 10. And I know you have promised to finish the novel which you are writing.

(Matriculation, June 1934)

1 § 47 (*e*). 2 'the red' (omit 'one'). 3 'that it is tomorrow Friday.' 4 *c'est pour cela que*. 5 § 78.

XXVI

1. Yesterday morning my wife was sewing in the garden because it was so hot indoors. 2. She dropped several pieces of cotton on the grass, and forgot to pick them up. 3. On looking through the window a few hours later, I noticed a small bird which was carrying them away. 4. It must have a nest in one of those trees. I hope we shall be able to find it. 5. Everything is so quiet here that the birds are not afraid to come near the house. 6. There are a great many of them, and their songs often wake us early. 7. We like to hear them singing, but the noise they make disturbs[1] our visitors. 8. One of our friends who spent a night here told me that they had prevented him from sleeping. 9. That surprised me, for they do not begin to sing before five o'clock. 10. He lives in London, and when he is at home he sleeps well in spite of the noises of the streets.

(Matriculation, September 1934)

1 Use *déranger*.

XXVII

1. Many[1] years ago there was a young man who lived with his wife in a little village near the mountains. 2. All the village children knew him well, because he often played with them and told them stories. 3. Unfortunately he did not like work, and his wife was always scolding[2] him, telling him that they would die of hunger. 4. To escape from his wife, he sometimes took his gun and went for a walk in the woods with his dog. 5. One day he had walked far,[3] and being tired, sat down under a tree to rest. 6. He stayed there for a long time. The scene[4] was very beautiful, for it was evening and the sun was setting. 7. Suddenly he heard someone calling him. He looked all round, but

at first saw no one. 8. His dog who had been sleeping[5] got up quickly and came to his master as if he were afraid. 9. Then an old man appeared, bent under the weight of something which he carried on his back. 10. Thinking it was one of his neighbours who needed help, the young man began to run towards him.

(Matriculation, September 1935)

1 § 3 (*a*). 2 § 76 (*a*). 3 'he had gone far.' 4 *la vue*.
5 Imperfect.

XXVIII

1. A learned professor was trying one evening to finish a chapter of his book. 2. He was finding it so difficult that he had forgotten to have his dinner. 3. He had told his wife never to disturb him when he was working. 4. Towards midnight, however, the poor lady dared to knock at the door of his room. 5. She asked him, in a timid voice, if he did not wish to have something to eat. 6. He replied that he would prepare a meal himself, when his chapter was[1] finished. 7. So his wife brought an egg, some bread and butter, and some water in a saucepan (*casserole*). 8. His work being finished at last, the professor got up and put the saucepan on the fire to heat the water. 9. He took his watch out of his pocket, in order to know when the egg would be ready. 10. A few minutes later he discovered that he was holding the egg and that his watch was boiling in the saucepan.

(Matriculation, January 1936)

1 Tense?

XXIX

1. One December evening my aunt was working at the college after all the students had gone.[1] 2. She went upstairs to fetch a book which she had left in a small library. 3. While she was looking for it she thought she heard[2] footsteps approaching. 4. She paid no attention to them,[3] but to her great surprise someone turned the key of the door. 5. She called out, but nobody answered. She knew that the porter[4] was a little deaf. 6. The idea of spending the whole night shut up in that room[5] was not at all pleasant. 7. She tried to attract the attention of the passers-by,[6] but the window was too high and it was already dark. 8. Then she wrote a note and threw it into the street, hoping that somebody would see it. 9. She waited a long time, but at last a lady picked up the note and read it. 10. She smiled at my aunt, rang at the gate, and within five minutes the prisoner was free.

(Matriculation, September 1936)

1 'after the departure of all the students.' 2 § 58 (*b*). 3 *y*. 4 *le portier*. 5 room, *la salle*. 6 *les passants*.

XXX

Some years ago I was travelling in France and stopped at a seaside town full of foreigners who had come there from all parts of the world.

As it was my first visit to the place, I left my luggage at the station and walked through the streets to look for[1] a lodging.

I soon came to a fairly clean little hotel, where my attention was immediately attracted by the following notice: 'English, Spanish, Italian, Russian, and German spoken here.'

Struck with astonishment, I entered and asked for the interpreter, although I hesitated to[2] disturb so[3] learned a man.—'There isn't one', the waiter calmly told me.

'Then who speaks all the languages advertised on your door?'—'Why, the visitors, Sir,' he replied with a smile. 'If you have lunch[4] here, you can hear them.'

(Cambridge Local School Certificate, December 1931)

1 *à la recherche de.* 2 *malgré mon hésitation à*+inf. 3 § 17 (*d*).
4 have lunch, *déjeuner.*

XXXI

A lady who was travelling in a railway carriage fell asleep. Presently she awoke, and, to pass the time, examined the contents of her handbag.

To her astonishment, she discovered she had lost a 500 franc note[1] and looked with suspicion at a well-dressed woman sitting in the corner opposite her.

While the latter was sleeping after lunch in her turn, the former saw the note in her neighbour's book and gently withdrew it.

On her arrival she found a telephone message awaiting her: 'Don't worry about the note; you left it on the drawing-room table.'

She was horror-stricken, but how could she restore the money she herself had stolen? What do you think she ought to have done?

(Cambridge Local School Certificate, July 1932)

1 the note, *le billet.*

XXXII

A famous French artist who was very absent-minded had just returned to Paris after travelling for several months in Switzerland.

As soon as he got home, he wrote letters to all his friends to invite them to dinner on Wednesday of the following week.

On that day the painter himself did his best to[1] ensure the comfort of his guests; he desired above all to satisfy everyone's taste.

When it struck seven o'clock[2] everything was ready, but, though the host waited an hour, nobody arrived.

Suddenly he had[3] an idea; he opened a drawer in his desk and discovered that he had forgotten to post the invitations.

(Cambridge Local School Certificate, July 1934)

1 § 81 (*b*). 2 'when seven o'clock struck.' 3 Tense?

XXXIII

A rich American decided to buy nothing at a sale which he had to attend. A charming girl offered him a cigarette-box.

He looked at it and shook his head.—'No, thanks,[1] I don't smoke.' 'A fountain pen, then?'[2]—'No,' he growled, 'I never write.'

Still[3] smiling, she handed[4] him a bottle of eau-de-cologne. —'I never use scent; you may keep that for the ladies.'

She began again: 'Here is a new kind of razor with which you cannot cut yourself.'—'I never shave myself, I go to the barber's.'

She stopped for a moment to reflect. Finally she begged him to accept a piece of soap. He could not say: 'I never wash.'— He bought it.

(Cambridge Local School Certificate, December 1934)

1 No, thanks, *Merci*. 2 *donc*. 3 *toujours*. 4 hand, *tendre*.

XXXIV

One winter's day a kind old gentleman whom I knew was stopped by a beggar at the entrance to a shop in Paris.

This man, who seemed to be poor, asked for money for his wife and children, and my friend gave him all that he had in his purse.

During the afternoon, he was surprised to see the beggar again; this time he was sitting near the door of a restaurant, drinking wine.

Before the gentleman had time to speak, he began to make excuses: 'Yes, I know what you must think of me.'

'I have not forgotten my family. But you who have had a good lunch will easily understand how much I was tempted.'

(Cambridge Local School Certificate, July 1935)

XXXV

A selfish young man was travelling from London to Scotland and wanted to lie down and sleep quietly on the way.

He arrived at the station early and placed all his bags on the seat,[1] to keep other travellers from disturbing him.

A stranger asked if all the places were taken. 'Yes', the young man replied. 'These things belong to my friends, who will be back soon.'

'They have gone to buy some tobacco.' However, the stranger got in and waited until the train started. Nobody came.

Then, knowing that the young man was lying, he remarked, 'I don't want your friends to lose their luggage', threw the bags on the platform, and sat down.

(Cambridge Local School Certificate, July 1936)

1 *la banquette.*

XXXVI

At last the trunks (*malle*, f.) were ready and the children dressed. At eleven they went off, leaving Mr Smith to lock up the house[1] and then[2] to follow them to the station. Just as he was starting, a man with a cart stopped at the door and said that Mrs Smith had been to his shop[3] and ordered him to fetch the carpets (*tapis*, m.) and to clean them during her absence. Mr Smith was surprised that his wife had not told[4] him her decision; but he knew that she often forgot things, and so he helped the man to put the carpets into his cart. That done, he hurried to the station. But when he spoke to his wife about it she did not seem to understand what he was talking about.[5] Soon, however, they guessed the truth. The man was a thief who had thus cleverly[6] robbed them of[7] their best carpets.

(Oxford Local School Certificate, December 1926)

1 'leaving to Mr Smith the care of locking up, etc.' 2 *ensuite*. 3 *passer chez lui*. 4 *communiquer*. 5 'what he meant (*vouloir dire*).' 6 *par cette ruse*. 7 § 18.

XXXVII

The old lady drew aside the curtain and looked out of the window. The first thing she noticed was that[1] her gate was open and that Miss Trimmer's brown cow had come in and was at that moment[2] peacefully eating her best flowers.[3] Next, as she was going to call the maid, she saw that the stable door was likewise open, although it was not yet a quarter to eight. At this moment Sarah ran into the room without knocking. 'Please, ma'am,' she said, 'there's a lady whom I do not know asleep on the sofa in the hall, and by her is[4] a dog who growls and shows his teeth every time I try to go near her! How can they have got in?'

(Oxford Local School Certificate, July 1927)

1 *ce fut que*. 2 *à cet instant précis*. 3 'was in the act of (*en train de* + inf.) eating peacefully her most beautiful flowers.' 4 *se trouve*.

XXXVIII

Mrs Brown was in the kitchen when her husband appeared. He had gone to town, where he had sold the butter and eggs which his wife had given him, and he held in his hand[1] a pair of gloves. Although he had bought them with his own money he thought that his wife would be angry, for she did not like gloves and already had one pair which she wore on Sundays[2] and another which she kept in a drawer of the wardrobe which stood[3] in her bedroom. But she did not seem to notice the gloves and went on with her work; so he placed them on the table and left the kitchen without telling her what he had bought. When he returned in the evening he saw that they were still where[4] he had left them.

(Oxford Local School Certificate, July 1929)

1 § 95 (*b*). 2 § 1 (*c*). 3 § 115 (*b*). 4 *à l'endroit où.*

XXXIX

Last week my brother went to France. He left on Monday and spent the night in London. Next morning he got up early and caught the ten o'clock train, which arrives at Newhaven about noon. At five in[1] the afternoon he landed at Dieppe and had a cup of coffee with some bread and butter before he got into the train. There was so much to see on the way[2] that the time passed very quickly, and he was astonished when he suddenly found that the train was crossing the Seine. At the station his friends, who had just arrived, were waiting for him. As soon as he alighted they saw him and came forward to help him with[3] his luggage. His wonderful week in Paris had begun.

(Oxford Local School Certificate, July 1930)

1 What preposition? 2 *en route.* 3 'to carry his luggage.'

XL

When I had got up and dressed, I heard someone coming[1] towards my door. It was the man whom I had seen the evening before when I awoke and found myself in prison. He told me to follow him into the courtyard where I might walk up and down for ten minutes before breakfast. I was very glad of this and asked him if there were other prisoners. He hesitated and then said that he did not think so,[2] but that he had just arrived himself to take the place of another man who was ill. But when I asked him how long the governor would keep me in prison he refused to answer and shook his head. I did not ask him any more questions, but at once began to walk, for it was very cold.

(Oxford Local School Certificate, December 1930)

1 § 49 (*b*). 2 § 29.

XLI

My dear friend,

I have not received a letter from you for[1] several weeks. What are you doing now? Has your brother returned from London? I hope you will soon be able to come and spend a week with me. If your sister can come too, my sister will be very pleased. My brother is still in France. He is enjoying himself and does not want to come back before Christmas, but my father has written to tell him that he must come home next month. He will have much to tell us when he returns,[2] I'm sure.[3] Write soon and tell me when you are[4] coming. Remember me to[5] your mother, please.

Yours sincerely,[6]

A. B.

(Oxford Local School Certificate, December 1931)

1 § 118 (*a*). 2 Tense? 3 'I am sure of it.' 4 Tense?
5 *Rappelez-moi au bon souvenir de.* 6 *Bien à vous.*

XLII

Use Perfect, not Past Definite.

Yesterday I went with several friends to the castle which is near our town. We set out at two o'clock in the afternoon. A path leads there through several fields and is much shorter than the road. We followed it as far as the village which takes its name from[1] the castle. There we rested for half an hour. Then we entered the park by the main gate. On our left there was a beautiful lake upon which swam a large number of[2] ducks. There was also a small boat in which sat[3] two men who were fishing. We decided to visit the apartments, which are open on Tuesdays,[4] Thursdays and Saturdays. During the winter months the castle is closed and visitors are admitted only to the park. When we arrived in the first room we found so many interesting things to see that the time passed very quickly. We decided to return another day and I hope you will accompany us.

(Oxford Local School Certificate, December 1932)

1 *porter le nom de*. 2 *bon nombre de* + plural verb. 3 'were sitting.' 4 § 1 (*c*).

XLIII

I was two years old when my parents died. My aunt consented to bring me up. She did not like children, but she was a poor widow and thought with satisfaction of the money which my parents had left me. She lived in a large ugly house which stood in the middle of a yard filled with mud, hens, and rabbits. It was[1] there that I was to spend the days of my childhood and youth. The village priest was charged with my education and he was the only person I could regard as a friend. He came three times a week[2] to give me lessons. He always carried his hat in his hand and smiled at the passers-by, the birds, the trees, the blades of grass. When he entered the yard, hens and rabbits gathered round him to pick up the crusts of bread which he had taken care to put in his pocket before setting out.

(Oxford Local School Certificate, July 1935)

1 *C'est*. 2 § 100 (*c*).

XLIV

It was almost midnight. The two travellers halted at the place where the path enters[1] the forest. It was so dark that they did not at first see a man who was sitting upon a heap of stones a few paces from[2] them. But he began to groan and then they noticed him. 'What is the matter?[3] What has happened to you?' said one of the travellers. 'I have been attacked by robbers, who have taken my money and a letter which I was taking to the town on[4] the other side of the forest. It was addressed to the governor of the province and contained a very important document. I advise you to return at once to the village you have just left, for I am sure that the robbers are still in the forest.' The travellers decided to follow his advice, and while one of them remained with him, the other returned to the village to warn the police and find a horse and cart.

(Oxford Local School Certificate, July 1936)

1 *s'engager dans*. 2 § 95 (*a*). 3 § 112. 4 *de*.

XLV

The King advanced quickly towards Eliza. 'Follow me,' said he, 'for you must not remain here, and if you are as good as you are beautiful, I will clothe you in silk and will place a crown of gold upon your head and you shall dwell in my palace.' With these words[1] he placed[2] the young girl upon his horse, and, as she continued to cry, said, 'Calm yourself, I will do you no harm.' They went off over[3] the high mountains and towards sunset arrived before a magnificent city which was situated in the middle of a valley. The King conducted the girl to the palace and ordered his servants[4] to bring precious garments and to clothe her as though she were already queen. When they had done what he had commanded they led her to the council-chamber, and when she entered, the King and all his subjects rose and the King declared that she should be his wife.

(Oxford Local School Certificate, December 1936)

1 'On saying these words.' 2 In this sentence only, 'place' should be translated by *faire monter*. 3 They went off over, *ils franchirent*. 4 *serviteurs*, m.

B. *ANECDOTES*

I

An American was sitting in a café in Spain. He had ordered some coffee and it had just been brought[1] to him. He then[2] wished to ask for some milk, but, not knowing how to[3] translate this word into Spanish, he did not succeed in making the waiter understand[4] what he wanted.[5]

Suddenly he had[6] an idea. He took[7] from his pocket a pencil and a sheet of paper and proceeded to draw a cow.

The waiter smiled, nodded to show that he had understood, and hurried out of the café.

He remained away a long time, and the American was beginning to wonder what had become of him,[8] when at last he returned and handed[9] to his astonished customer a ticket for a bull fight.

1 Avoid passive by using *on*. 2 *ensuite*. 3 § 82. 4 § 60 (*b*). 5 *vouloir*. 6 Tense? 7 *tirer*. 8 § 119. 9 *remettre*.

II

On[1] a fine summer day a traveller was making his way along[2] a lonely road. The heat was stifling and he was beginning to get very tired. At nightfall he arrived in front of an inn with the sign of[3] George and the Dragon. As he was very hot and very thirsty, he decided to stop to have a drink.[4] He knocked at the door of the inn, but for[5] some time no one replied. After waiting in vain for the door to be opened[6] he knocked again. This time a ferocious-looking woman put her head out of the window and asked him what he wanted. 'A drink',[7] replied the traveller. 'Go away,' she cried, 'or I'll set[8] the dogs on you.' 'Well, in that case, kindly tell[9] George I should like a word with him.'[10]

1 § 100. 2 *cheminer sur.* 3 *à l'enseigne de.* 4 *boire un coup.* 5 § 101. 6 § 88. 7 *À boire.* 8 *lâcher.* 9 *prévenir.* 10 *lui dire un mot.*

III

On a certain railway line the local train used to make long stops at every little station all along the line. During these stops the passengers did not fail to make fun of the station master. They put their heads[1] out of the window and asked him for leave to get out and pick the flowers. They amused themselves by repeating this request at every station where the train stopped.

At last one of them, realising that the joke was getting[2] a little stale, went one better.[3] To those who were asking for leave to pick the flowers the station master had just replied that they would hardly find any[4] at that season of the year.

'Don't worry about that,' retorted the wag, 'I've brought a packet of seeds.'

1 § 1 (*h*). 2 *devenir.* 3 *trouva quelque chose de mieux.* 4 § 6 (*a*).

IV

There was once a man of wit who was very fond of travelling. He generally went on foot. During one of his journeys he came to[1] a German town and lodged at the best inn he could find.[2] Soon however he had no money left, and in order to get more,[3] he went round the town to announce a wonderful show which would be open to the public on the following day.

'Come', said he, 'and see the strangest horse that ever lived.[4] Its tail is where[5] its head ought to be.'

The people came in crowds to see this strange sight, but on entering the stable where the animal was to be found,[6] they discovered just an ordinary horse[7] with its tail tied fast to the manger. The folk could not help laughing at the way[8] they had been deceived,[9] but they took care not to reveal the secret to those who had not yet come in.

1 *arriver dans.* 2 Mood? 3 'to have more (*davantage*) of it.' 4 Mood? 5 *à l'endroit où.* 6 *se trouvait.* 7 *un cheval quelconque.* 8 *la façon dont.* 9 Avoid the passive by using *on*.

V

Penny Postage

After writing a letter, a gentleman rang for the servant to take it to the post office. As the servant had gone out on an errand, and[1] the letter was urgent, the gentleman prepared to post it himself. While he put on his coat and hat, his little six years' old boy came running up to[2] him and begged to be allowed[3] to post it himself. His father gave him the letter and a penny to buy a stamp. He set off highly pleased. When he had been away a long time, the father grew anxious and went in search of his son. The boy ran eagerly up to him[4] and said, 'Oh, father,[5] I waited, and I saw a lot of men putting[6] letters into a small hole. When no one was looking I slipped yours through for nothing.[7] Here is the penny'; and the child handed back the coin to his astonished father.

1 § 33. 2 § 48. 3 § 87. 4 'ran towards him eagerly (*d'un air empressé*).' 5 *papa.* 6 § 49 (*c*). 7 'without paying anything.'

VI

The Deaf Man's Story

Some gentlemen were sitting at dinner. One of them told a funny story which made everyone laugh.[1] The gentleman at whose table[2] they were dining was very deaf, and could not hear a word of it. But he did not like people to know[3] how deaf he was,[4] so he laughed at the same time as the others, and said it was a very funny story indeed.[5] When the laughter had subsided, the deaf man remarked that he knew a much funnier story. All the guests said they would like to hear it. So the deaf gentleman told his story, and made them laugh more than ever.[6] But he did not know what they were laughing at.[7] Instead of laughing at his story, they were laughing because, without knowing it, he had told the very same story that had just been[8] related.

1 § 60 (*a*). 2 *chez qui.* 3 § 84; people, *on.* 4 Order of words in French? 5 § 4 (*d*). 6 *de plus belle.* 7 § 12 (*b*). 8 Avoid passive.

VII

How to Avoid Sea-sickness

A gentleman, who had often suffered from sea-sickness, believed that he had found[1] a way to[2] avoid it by going to bed as soon as he came on board,[3] and remaining there until he arrived at his destination. The next time he had to make a journey by sea he lost no time in climbing into his berth, and in a few minutes was fast asleep, and slept like a top until seven o'clock next morning. He arose delighted, satisfied that he had[4] at last found a remedy for the disorder[5] which had made him suffer so much. Going on[6] deck with a satisfied look on his face, he met the captain. He at once exclaimed, 'My remedy has been completely successful. I haven't had the slightest sea-sickness all night.'[7] The captain smiled.[8] 'What are you laughing for?' he asked, in surprise.[9] 'Because', was the answer, 'the ship has been in dock all night. She[10] has not stirred a foot.'

1 § 58 (*b*). 2 *le moyen de*. 3 § 36. 4 *satisfait de*+inf. 5 *au mal*. 6 *monter sur*. 7 § 97 (*b*). 8 Say 'And the captain smiled' and use the historic infinitive (§ 73). 9 Say 'surprised' (*surpris*). 10 Remember that 'ship' is masculine in French.

VIII

A True Story

Lady X. entered a shop to buy a pair of gloves as a Christmas present for her son. On returning home she discovered that a gold ring, set with diamonds, was missing.[1] A long search was made,[2] but no one succeeded in finding it. Soon afterwards a gentleman received a pair of gloves as a Christmas present. While putting on one of these gloves he found an obstruction of some kind lodged in the little finger.[3] He turned the glove inside out and found in it a gold ring set with diamonds. At first he thought that the ring must belong to his sister-in-law, who had sent him the gloves, but on learning that it did not belong to her, he had it despatched to the shop where she had bought them. As soon as the manager of the shop received it, he sent a wire to Lady X. informing her that the ring had been found. On receipt of[4] the wire she immediately repaired to the shop, and the manager handed over to her the ring, which had got caught in[5] the little finger of the glove, just as she was putting it on.

1 'that there was missing (*il lui manquait*)', followed by subject. 2 Avoid the passive. 3 'that something was obstructing (*boucher*) the little finger.' 4 *au reçu de*. 5 get caught in, *se loger dans*.

IX

A Hockey Match

A hockey match was about to be played[1] at Muddleton-in-the-Marsh.[2] Unfortunately one of the two teams turned up on the ground[3] without a goalkeeper, and it became necessary to find a substitute. A young man was chosen[4] among the spectators and provided with a club.

In vain did he protest[5] that he knew nothing about hockey, he was told that it didn't matter at all,[6] all he had to do was to prevent the ball from passing between the posts.

The game[7] began and attacks were frequently made[8] against the goal where the young man was stationed. It soon became clear that he had told the truth and that he did not shine at hockey. When half-time arrived, he had already let the ball through six times. 'Idiot!' cried the captain indignantly, 'couldn't you have made an effort to stop some of those balls?' 'Why,[9] of course,' replied the young man, 'but what is the good of stopping them, when you have a net on purpose to do it?'

1 'was going to be played (*se jouer*).' 2 *Fouilly-les-Oies*. 3 *le terrain*. 4 Avoid the passive. 5 § 57. 6 'that that had no importance.' 7 *la partie*. 8 *se multiplièrent*. 9 *Mais*.

X

There was no mistake about it,[1] the train was late.[2] The passengers, who had been awaiting[3] its arrival for more than an hour and a half, complained bitterly about it, and one of them, who was afraid he would miss[4] an appointment, went and lodged a complaint with[5] the station master. The latter tried to appease his wrath by explaining to him that circumstances outside the control of[6] the Company were responsible for the delay. He pointed out to him that the train had had to[7] stop at several places along the line[8] and that in consequence of these stops, it had lost time between the stations. He went so far as to[9] demonstrate that by[10] his watch, which showed[11] Greenwich time, the train was not so late as[12] the complainer asserted.

But the indignant passenger was not to be put off so easily.[13] 'You can't explain things in that way,' said he. 'What you want is[14] not a watch, it's a calendar.'

1 § 79. 2 § 111 (*b*). 3 § 38 (*a*). 4 § 65. 5 *auprès de.* 6 'which did not depend on.' 7 § 54 (*e*). 8 *le long du parcours.* 9 § 81 (*d*). 10 What preposition? 11 *marquer.* 12 § 111 (*b*). 13 *ne se laissa pas désarçonner pour si peu.* 14 § 16 (*a*).

XI

Tit for Tat

(*A bon Chat bon Rat*)

A tennis tournament was about to[1] take place on the Riviera. A young man, who had already entered for the gentlemen's singles, had just finished a practice game with a famous lady player as partner.

At the end of the set he went up to her and invited her to enter with him for the mixed doubles. To which[2] the lady replied, 'I am very sorry to disappoint you, but my uncle[3] always gets my partners for me.' The young man, though[4] naturally annoyed, said nothing. As it was only too evident that the lady did not consider him a good enough player to be[5] her partner, he thought it best to[6] remain silent.[7]

Two years later, when his game had much improved, he found himself once more playing[8] with the same lady. At the end of the set she went up to him and asked him to enter with her for the mixed doubles. 'I'm awfully sorry not to be able to oblige you,'[9] he replied, 'but my aunt always gets me my partners.'

1 'was going to.' 2 § 12 (*a*). 3 'it is my uncle who.' 4 § 90 (*c*). 5 § 81 (*b*). 6 § 69 (*a*). 7 *garder le silence.* 8 'it happened to him again (*de nouveau*) to play.' 9 *vous faire ce plaisir.*

XII

A False Alarm

One evening Monsieur Dupont returned home very late.[1] Reaching[2] the front door, he was just going to put the key in the lock when he heard a deep bass voice shouting, 'Don't come in or I shoot.' Monsieur Dupont hesitated a moment,[3] then he made a dash for the police station. 'Inspector,'[4] said he, 'Arm your men. There is a burglar in my house who is threatening to kill anyone who approaches him.'

No sooner said than done.[5] The policemen take their revolvers and accompany Monsieur Dupont to his house. They invite the supposed burglar to surrender. Finding his replies incomprehensible they burst open the door. And what do they find? A desperate burglar? No, the wireless set of Monsieur Dupont which he had forgotten to turn off and which was continuing its harangue[6] in stentorian tones, 'And that, my dear listeners, is[7] the end of the second adventure of Arsène Lupin. We are now closing down till 10 o'clock tomorrow morning.[8] Good night, Mesdames. Good night, Mesdemoiselles. Good night, Messieurs.'

1 'returned (*rentrer*) very late to his house (*chez lui*).' 2 *Arrivé devant*. 3 § 43. 4 *Monsieur l'Inspecteur*. 5 § 105. 6 *poursuivre sa harangue*. 7 that...is, *voilà*. 8 Say 'our next transmission will take place at 10 o'clock', etc.

XIII

A Slight Mistake

A young man had just become enrolled as a member of a Golf Club. Before beginning his round, he asked the secretary for a scoring card, saying that he was going round[1] alone and wished to make a careful record of[2] the number of his strokes. The secretary gave him the card and the young man made his way to[3] the first teeing ground.

On his return to the pavilion, after completing his round, he looked quite gay, and when the secretary asked him how he had got on,[4] he proudly replied: 'I have done the round in five under[5] bogey.' 'That's splendid',[6] said the secretary. 'May I see your card?' The young man handed it over to him and the other, after glancing at it, could not help laughing. 'My friend,' said he, 'I'm afraid you've made a mistake. Those numbers that you see on the card are not bogey's, they show[7] the distances between the holes.'

1 *faire un parcours.* 2 *tenir un compte exacte.* 3 *se diriger vers.* 4 *s'en tirer.* 5 *en cinq de moins que.* 6 § 16 (*e*). 7 *indiquer.*

XIV

The shopman uses *tu* in speaking to the boy, but the boy uses *vous* in speaking to the shopman.

A little boy entered a shop and asked the shopman for a pennyworth of milk in a glass. On receiving it he held it a moment in his hand, while he looked longingly at some buns on the counter.[1]

'Can I exchange my glass of milk for a penny bun?'

'Certainly', said the shopman, taking back[2] the milk and giving him the bun. The boy was just going out when the shopman called him back.

'Hi, there![3] You haven't paid.'

'Paid for what?'

'Why,[4] the bun.'

'I gave you a glass of milk for it.'[5]

'But you didn't pay for the glass of milk.'

'Of course not.[6] I gave it back to you.'

When the puzzled shopman had finished scratching his head, the little boy had disappeared.

1 'which were (*se trouvaient*) on the counter.' 2 Insert 'from him'. 3 *Hé, là-bas.* 4 *Mais.* 5 *en échange.* 6 Omit 'not'.

XV

I heard a voice cry 'Stop!'[1] and a figure on horseback approached the chaise. Before letting down the window,[2] I had[3] the presence of mind to take my watch out of my pocket and stuff it in my waistcoat under my arm. 'Your purses and your watches!' cried the highwayman. 'I have no watch!' I replied. 'Then your purse!' I gave it to him. It contained nine guineas. It was so dark that I could not see his hand, but I felt him take it. He then asked for Lady Browne's purse, saying: 'Don't be frightened, I will not hurt you.' 'You won't frighten the lady?' 'No, I give you my word.[4] I will do her no hurt.'

Lady Browne gave him her purse and was going to add her watch, but he said, 'I am much obliged to you', pulled off his hat, and rode away.

'Well, Lady Browne,' said I, 'another time you won't be afraid of being robbed?' 'Oh, but I am afraid', said she. 'I am in terror lest[5] he should return, for I have given him a purse containing only bad money,[6] which I carry on purpose.'[7]

1 *Halte!* 2 *la glace.* 3 Tense? 4 *parole*, f. 5 *être dans la frayeur que...ne*+subj. 6 *la fausse monnaie.* 7 *exprès.*

XVI

A Weather Report

An old lady, who lived in a little village in the country,[1] found herself under[2] the necessity of making a journey to London. On arriving at the terminus she asked the porter to find her a taxi. As it was the first time she had travelled[3] in a taxi, she took care to select a staid and sedate-looking driver,[4] and, before she got in, she requested him not to go too fast. 'Don't be afraid, Madam,' he replied, 'I'll take good care not to.'[5] Thus reassured the old lady got in and sat down. After a few moments[6] she noticed that, from time to time, the driver was holding out his right hand to signal to the following traffic.[7] Not understanding this gesture, she became more and more uneasy. At last, unable to restrain herself any longer,[8] 'Hi, mister,'[9] she cried in a decisive tone, 'You look after[10] the car. I'll tell you when it stops[11] raining.'

1 *en province.* 2 *dans.* 3 say 'was travelling'. 4 'a driver of staid and sedate appearance (*aspect*).' 5 *je m'en garderai bien.* 6 *au bout de quelques instants.* 7 'the cars (*voitures*) which were coming behind.' 8 *n'y tenant plus.* 9 *Dites donc, vous.* 10 Insert *donc* after the imperative. 11 Tense?

XVII

Mr Balfour at New York

'Mr Balfour, we want you to[1] see our new Woolworth Buildings,[2] before you leave New York.'

'Delighted.'

The appointment made,[3] Mr Balfour and his American friend take up their stand[4] opposite the enormous skyscraper.

'Now,[5] Mr Balfour, you see before you the greatest building in[6] the world. It has fifty storeys, and in the day-time it houses four hundred principals and three thousand clerks.'

'Remarkable!' said Mr Balfour, after scanning the building through[7] his glasses.

'It is nine hundred feet high[8] and it was constructed from the basement to the summit[9] in[10] one year and eight months.'

Mr Balfour, after gazing at the building again, 'Really!'

'It is built entirely of[11] steel and concrete and it is non-inflammable.'[12]

Mr Balfour, after a third survey, 'Wh...what a pity!'

1 § 84. 2 *bâtiments Woolworth.* 3 *Rendez-vous pris.* 4 *se plantent.* 5 *Voilà.* 6 § 97 (*c*). 7 *avec.* 8 § 97 (*e*). 9 *depuis le sous-sol jusqu'au faîte.* 10 § 99 (*b*). 11 *en.* 12 *complètement à l'épreuve du feu.*

XVIII

A Spare Umbrella

A season ticket holder used to journey every day to London, armed with[1] the neatly rolled umbrella which is the pride[2] of the city man. Now[3] it happened that one day he left the umbrella in town to have it repaired. The next morning he made his usual journey[4] to[5] the City and, on arriving at the terminus, he inadvertently took another traveller's umbrella from[6] the rack.

As soon as he realised[7] his mistake, he apologised profusely and restored the article to its owner.

This incident ruffled him, and to avoid any repetition of the offence[8] he took the precaution of buying a spare umbrella[9] when he went to fetch the one that was being repaired.[10] Imagine his confusion when, on getting into the railway carriage for[11] his return journey, he found there the subject[12] of his contretemps of the morning, who greeted him with a smile and quietly remarked,[13] 'Well, you didn't do so badly[14] after all!'

1 *nanti de.* 2 *fait l'orgueil.* 3 *Or.* 4 'the usual journey (*trajet*, m.).' 5 *vers.* 6 *dans.* Cf. *prendre dans sa poche, boire dans un verre.* 7 *s'apercevoir de.* 8 any repetition of the offence, *toute récidive.* 9 *un parapluie de réserve.* 10 being repaired, *en réparation.* 11 'to make.' 12 *le témoin.* 13 *fit tout doucement.* 14 *s'en tirer trop mal.*

XIX

Use 2nd Person Singular throughout.

M. Dupont had just bought a second-hand car, which was said to be very fast.[1] Shortly afterwards he took his little son Jeannot for a ride. 'Jeannot,' said M. Dupont, 'I want to see how fast this car will go.[2] Look out of the window at the back,[3] and directly you see a man in[4] a blue suit, wearing a silver badge, let me know[5] at once.'

Little Jeannot promised to obey his father's instructions. He turned round and kept his nose[6] glued to the back window, watching for the man in blue, while his father trod on the accelerator. M. Dupont went faster and faster,[7] the speedometer marked thirty, forty, fifty miles an hour.[8] Time went by, but little Jeannot did not open his lips. At last, after a long chase, a policeman, riding a motor bicycle, succeeded in getting abreast of[9] the car. Then little Jeannot turned to his father and with a satisfied smile, 'Here he is, papa', said he. 'Here's the man you are looking for.'

1 § 59. 2 'what speed this car can attain (*atteindre*).' 3 *la vitre de derrière.* 4 *en.* 5 *prévenir.* 6 *se tint le nez....* 7 § 109. 8 *à l'heure.* 9 *se mettre à la hauteur de.*

XX

An airman offered to take a young lady for a trip[1] in an aeroplane. She replied that she would accept his offer, if he promised to be careful. 'Don't be afraid,' said he, 'I'm sure you will be delighted with your trip.' 'I'll tell you that when we come down', she answered, as she got into the cabin.

The airman started up the engine, the propellers began to turn and the machine took off. But as soon as it had gained height, the pilot began to perform all kinds of stunts.[2] He looped the loop so many times that his companion nearly[3] died of fright. At last he decided to come down. The machine landed and the young lady got out of the cabin. When the airman asked her how she had enjoyed the trip, she replied, 'I told you I would answer that when we came down. Well, I wish[4] to thank you for my two flights. I shall never forget them.' 'What? two flights? Why you've only had[5] one.' 'Don't you make any mistake,[6] my friend, I've had two. My first and my last.'[7]

1 'offered to a young lady to (*de*+inf.) take her for a trip.' 2 *faire toutes sortes d'acrobaties.* 3 § 57. 4 *tenir à*+inf. 5 have, *faire.* 6 *Détrompez-vous.* 7 'the first and the last.'

C. *ORIGINAL PASSAGES*

I

It is Christmas morning. Madame Paillasse is sitting at the table.[1] There are also little Jean,[2] little Suzanne and little Pierre. With them[3] is[4] Monsieur Paillasse. He is not little. He is reading a paper. Why is Monsieur Paillasse reading a paper?[5] Does he not comprehend that it is Christmas Day? Certainly he comprehends. Then why does Monsieur Paillasse read the paper on[6] Christmas Day? It is not polite to ask[7] too many questions.

Punch

1 *à table.* 2 § 1 (*g*). 3 § 9 (*a*). 4 is, *se trouve.* 5 For interrogative form see § 28. 6 § 1 (*b*). 7 § 26.

II

Attention! The bell rings. Is it[1] the postman? Yes, it is[1] the postman. He always rings twice on Christmas Day. Run, Suzanne! Run, Pierre! Go and see[2] what[3] the kind postman has brought. He has brought letters and cards. Let us open them.

Madame Paillasse has received a card. What is there on the beautiful card of Madame Paillasse? I will tell you.[4] There is some holly, some snow, and some mistletoe. There are also a number of[5] robins, some bells, and a parrot. Why is there[6] a parrot on the card of Madame Paillasse? I couldn't tell you.[7]

Punch

1 § 24. 2 § 58 (*a*). 3 § 16 (*a*). 4 'I am going to tell it to you.' 5 *bon nombre de.* 6 § 27. 7 § 56.

III

Look! Jean has an engine, which runs by itself![1] When he winds it with a key, it runs along the table. Quick! there has been an accident. Jean's engine has struck the milk-jug. No matter.[2] There is plenty of milk in the kitchen. Wind up[3] your engine again, Jean. Aha! Now it has struck the tea-pot. Jean's engine runs well, does it not,[4] Monsieur Paillasse? Little Pierre has a trumpet. He is very pleased with it. Who has given Pierre such a[5] lovely trumpet? It is a present from Uncle Jacques. Is it not[6] kind of Uncle Jacques to send[7] Pierre such a lovely trumpet?

Punch

1 *toute seule.* 2 *n'importe.* 3 2nd pers. sing. 4 *n'est-ce pas?* 5 § 17 (*d*). 6 Is it not...? *N'est-ce pas que c'est...?* 7 § 69 (*b*).

IV

Monsieur Paillasse desires[1] some butter. Even on[2] Christmas Day one cannot do without butter. But where is it? On the table there is much paper. How can one find the butter when there is so much paper on the table? The butter has disappeared. No, here it is. It was under the box in which the engine of Jean was packed. It is full of sawdust. Come,[3] my children, pass[4] the butter to your father.

And Monsieur Paillasse? Has he not any presents? Yes, he has twelve golf balls, a box of cigars, and three ties. Monsieur Paillasse does not smoke and does not play golf,[5] but he wears ties.

Punch

1 *vouloir.* 2 § 1 (*b*). 3 *Allons.* 4 *faites passer.* 5 *jouer au golf.*

V

Autres Temps, Autres Mœurs

English women have[1] so many little meals. Before getting up in the morning they begin by drinking[2] a cup of tea with slices of bread and butter. Breakfast is a big meal of several courses, which takes place about nine o'clock. About eleven o'clock, for fear of[3] getting hungry, they eat a few biscuits and drink coffee. At one o'clock they have a big meal which is called lunch. Two or three hours later they are again hungry, so they go to a teashop and eat many cakes and drink a few cups of tea. In spite of that they have always a good appetite for dinner. After dinner they go to the theatre. On[4] coming out of the theatre they go and have supper in a restaurant. Between meals they drink little glasses of liqueurs. They say[5] that this fashion comes from America.

Punch

1 Look up 'have' in Gen. Vocab. 2 § 81 (*e*). 3 § 81 (*a*). 4 § 47 (*c*). 5 *on*+sing. verb.

VI

The Christmas Letter

Use the 2nd Person Singular throughout

Mother. Have you written to Aunt Mary to thank her for her present?

Child. No, I haven't written to her yet.

M. Well, have you written to Uncle George?

C. Not yet. The others haven't written either.[1]

M. Well, sit down and write at once.

C. But I don't know what to say.[2]

M. Say 'Dear Aunt Mary, Thank you so much[3] for the present you so kindly sent me.[4] I like it very much. Your affectionate niece, Joan.'

C. Can't I do it after lunch?

M. No.

C. Now I can't find anything to write with.[5]

M. What has become of[6] your fountain pen?

C. Someone must have[7] stolen it. I'll go and look for it after lunch.

M. No. Here's another pen. You must write to her at once.

C. Very well. Please may I write upstairs? The others have got the wireless on.[8] I shall be able to write much easier, if there's a noise going on.[9]

E.M.D. *Punch*

1 § 6 (*e*). 2 § 82. 3 Translate 'so much' by *beaucoup*. 4 'which you have had the kindness to send me.' 5 § 82. 6 § 119. 7 § 54 (*d*). 8 *faire de la T.S.F.* 9 'if one (*on*) makes a noise.'

VII

A Modern Fairy-tale (1)

The sun was at its highest[1] when he came to a thick wood and in its shade[2] he lay down to rest.[3] He was awakened by the[4] sound of sobs. Rising hastily to his feet, he peered through the trees and there, fifty yards from him, sitting on the bank of a stream, was the most beautiful damsel he had[5] ever seen, wringing her hands and weeping bitterly.

Prince Charming, grieved by the sight of beauty in distress, coughed and came nearer.

'Princess', he said tenderly, for he knew she was a Princess. 'You are in trouble. How can I help you?'

'Fair sir,' she answered, 'I had thought to be alone.[6] But since you are here, you can help me. I have a...a brother....'

But Prince Charming was not interested in brothers. So the Princess took him by the hand and led him into a clearing in the middle of the forest. Then she made him sit down[7] beside her on the grass and there she told him her tale.

A. A. Milne

1 *à son zénith*. 2 'in the shade of which.' 3 *prendre du repos*. 4 'a sound.' 5 § 93. 6 'I thought I was alone.' § 58 (*b*). 7 § 60 (*a*).

VIII

A Modern Fairy-tale (2)

'There is a giant called Blunderbuss,' said she, 'who lives[1] in a great castle ten miles from here. He is a terrible magician. Some years ago, because I would not marry him, he turned my brother into a.... I don't know how to tell you[2]...into a tortoise.' She raised[3] her hands to her face and sobbed again.[4]

'Why a tortoise?' said Prince Charming, knowing that sympathy was useless, but feeling that it was necessary[5] to say something.

'I don't know. He just thought of it.'[6]

'But why did he turn your brother into a tortoise.... I mean, if he had turned you yourself into one[7]...of course,' he added hurriedly, 'I am very glad he didn't do it.'

'Thank you', said Beauty.[8]

'But I don't understand why...'

'Oh, what does it matter why[9] he did it? Why do giants do things? I don't know.'

'Princess,' said Prince Charming, as he kissed her hand, 'Tell me how I can help you.' A. A. MILNE

1 *demeurer*. 2 'tell it to you.' For construction see § 82. 3 *porter*. 4 'began again to sob.' 5 Insert *bien* after 'it was necessary'. 6 *Ça lui est venu à l'idée comme ça*. 7 Omit 'into one'. 8 *La Belle*. 9 'What matters (*qu'importe*) the reason for which.'

IX

A Modern Fairy-tale (3)

'My brother', said Beauty,[1] 'was to meet me[2] here. He is late again,' she sighed, 'and he used to be so punctual.'

'But how can I help him?'

'I will tell you.[3] The only way to break the spell is to[4] kill the giant. Once the spell has remained for seven years, it remains for ever.' Here she looked down and burst into tears. 'The seven years are over[5] this evening at sunset.'

'I see', said Prince Charming thoughtfully.

'Here is my brother', cried Beauty.

An enormous tortoise came slowly into view.[6] Beauty rushed up to him, and having explained the situation, made the necessary introduction.

'Charmed', said the Tortoise. 'You can't mistake the castle, it's the only one near here,[7] and Blunderbuss is sure to be at home. I have no need to tell you how grateful I shall be to you if you will[8] kill him, but I am curious to know how you are going to set about it.'

'I have a friend here, who will help me', said Charming, fingering his ring. A. A. MILNE

1 *La Belle.* 2 *m'avait donné rendez-vous.* 3 'I am going to tell it to you.' 4 *c'est de*+inf. 5 'will be over (*terminé*).' 6 'appeared, advancing with (*à*) slow steps.' 7 'which is (*se trouve*) near here.' 8 *si vous voulez bien.*

X

The carter wrapped her bare feet in a piece of cloth and gave her some bread and some bacon and was very nice to her. But she was very cold and she felt very sad.

At last, at nightfall, after going a long way,[1] they saw the light shining[2] in the woodman's cottage and they went in. He was an old man and his children were having supper,[3] when their elder brother arrived with the cart. They jumped up immediately, clapping[4] their hands, for they were good children and their brother had brought them toys from the town. When they saw the fair stranger, they ran towards her and made her sit[5] near[6] the fire and rubbed her feet and brought her warm[7] bread and milk.

'Look,[8] father,' they cried, 'look what an odd[9] cloak she is wearing, just like the piece of velvet that hangs[10] in our cupboard, and round her neck she wears a little shoe just like the one you brought back from the forest—a little shoe of blue velvet.'

THACKERAY, *The Rose and the Ring*

1 go a long way, *faire un bon bout de chemin.* 2 Mood? § 49 (*a*). 3 have supper, *souper*. For construction see § 38 (*b*). 4 *en*+pres. part. 5 § 60 (*a*). 6 *auprès de.* 7 *bien chauds* after the nouns. 8 2nd pers. sing. 9 § 3 (*f*). 10 *est suspendu.*

XI

Monsieur Fracas cannot find[1] his car. His new car has been stolen from him[2] in the streets of Cairo. He has entered[3] the coiffeur's to have his beard trimmed,[4] and when he has emerged, his car had disappeared. Monsieur Fracas is in despair. Is it not a new car for which he has paid more than two hundred pounds? The impudence of the thieves makes him boil with rage. An example shall be made.[5] Monsieur Fracas rushes to the nearest police station.

A large policeman is sitting at a table.

'Quick,' shouts Monsieur Fracas, waving his arms in the face of[6] the policeman, 'my car, my new car, they have stolen it from me. Summon immediately[7] the Flying Squad, let them[8] set out in pursuit of[9] the thieves.'

The policeman does not leap to his feet. He does not shout[10] instructions down the telephone.[11] He does not even turn pale. He regards Monsieur Fracas with the utmost calm and takes out from[12] his desk Government Form No. 511263. *Punch*

1 *ne retrouve plus*. 2 § 20. 3 *entrer chez*. 4 § 60 (*d*). 5 § 17 (*b*). 6 *gesticuler au nez de*. 7 *sur-le-champ*. 8 *on*. 9 *se mettre à la poursuite de*. 10 *vociférer*. 11 *au téléphone*. 12 *sortir de* (transitive).

XII

'Be good enough,'[1] he says coldly, 'to answer a few questions. What is your name?'

'Jules Fracas.'

'Your age and the name and address of your father.'

'Ah! non', shouts Monsieur Fracas. 'I will sign your autograph album at a more convenient moment. At present it is a question of thieves. They are already half-way to Alexandria.'

At this thought Monsieur Fracas is on the point of tears,[2] but the policeman remains unmoved.

'Never mind,'[3] he says, 'understand that, with[4] the police, everything must be in order.'[5] Relentlessly he asks Monsieur Fracas his profession, the name and the profession of his father, his wife's name and the number of his children. He fills two large pages with information before he lays down his pen. Then he takes the document to the officer in charge. Monsieur Fracas waits for his return. At last the door opens and the policeman reappears. Monsieur Fracas observes that he is no longer calm.

'God be praised, you are still here",[6] he cries excitedly. 'There is one question that I have forgotten to ask you. The man who stole the car—what is his name and that of his father?' *Punch*

1 *avoir la bonté de*+inf. 2 'of weeping.' 3 *Ça ne fait rien.* 4 *dans.* 5 *en règle.* 6 *encore là.*

XIII

It was very cold weather and the ground was covered with snow. Giglio, who had given the name of Mr Giles, was very glad to find a comfortable seat inside the coach, where he sat next to[1] a woman carrying a bag. She appeared to be a very agreeable, well-informed and entertaining person. They travelled together till night and she gave Giglio all sorts of things out of[2] her bag, which seemed to contain the most wonderful collection of articles.[3] He was thirsty, and there came out of it[4] a bottle of beer and a silver mug. He was hungry, and she took out of it some cold chicken, some slices of ham, bread, salt, and a delicious piece of plum pudding.

During the journey,[5] the woman spoke to Giglio of many things, which he knew very little about.[6]

'My dear Mr Giles,' said she, 'you are a young man and the future belongs to[7] you. You must improve yourself and prepare for the day, when[8] you are[9] needed at home.'[10]

THACKERAY, *The Rose and the Ring*

1 *à côté de.* 2 out of, *provenant de.* 3 *objets*, m. 4 *il en sortit.* 5 *le trajet.* 6 'of which he was very ignorant.' 7 belongs to, *est à.* 8 § 11 (*b*). 9 'one (*on*) has need of you.' Tense? 10 *à la maison.*

XIV

'I advise you to stay[1] in the town, where the coach stops for the night. Remain there[2] and study,[3] and remember your old friend,[4] to whom you have been kind.'

'And who is my old friend?' asked Giglio.

'When you need[5] anything', said the lady, 'look in this bag, which I leave you as a present, and be grateful to—'

'To whom, Madam?'

'To the fairy Blackstick',[6] said the lady, flying out of[7] the window, and when Giglio asked the conductor who the lady was—

'What lady?' said the man. 'There hasn't been any[8] lady in the coach, except the old woman who got out at the last stage.'

Giglio thought he was dreaming,[9] but the bag, which the fairy had given him, was there,[10] lying on his knees, and when he arrived at the town, he took it in his hand and went into the inn.

THACKERAY, *The Rose and the Ring*

1 *séjourner.* 2 *y.* 3 *à étudier.* 4 Feminine. 5 Tense? 6 *la fée à la Baguette Noire.* 7 *s'envoler par.* 8 § 3 (*c*). 9 § 58 (*b*). 10 *là.*

XV

After the Children's Party

Did you enjoy yourselves at the party, my dears?[1]

Oh, yes. Is it supper time yet?[2]

Tell me who were there.[3]

Oh, any amount of people. Will you have time to read to us[4] before supper?

Yes, I'll come upstairs and read to you. Did you remember to say 'thank you' to Mrs Smith?

Yes. Only I'm not sure if I said it to the right lady.[5] There were so many people there.[6]

Well, there's the supper bell.[7] You'd better run away, dears. I'll come upstairs presently. I'm so glad it was[8] a nice party.

Oh, it was marvellous. Have we[9] to go to any other parties these holidays?[10]

I don't think so.[11] But...

Good.[12]

But I thought you enjoyed yourselves?

Oh, yes. There were tomato sandwiches and I ate them all.

Didn't any one else eat any?[13]

I don't know. Isn't it nearly[14] supper time? E.M.D. *Punch*

1 *mes chéris.* 2 'Is it yet (*enfin*) supper time?' 3 'who there were.' 4 *nous faire la lecture.* 5 *la dame qu'il fallait.* 6 Omit 'there'. 7 *voilà qu'on sonne pour le souper.* 8 *que ç'ait été.* 9 *Faudra-t-il que*+subj. 10 'during these holidays.' 11 § 29. 12 *à la bonne heure.* 13 § 6 (*c*). 14 *enfin.*

XVI

Use the Past Definite, not the Perfect.

We arrived at Waterloo at eleven o'clock and asked which platform the 11.15[1] started from. Of course nobody knew. The porter, who took our baggage, thought it would start from No. 2,[2] while another, whom I asked the same question, had heard that[3] it would start from No. 5. On the other hand the stationmaster was convinced it would start from the local platform.

Then our porter had[4] an idea. He said he thought it was to[5] start from No. 6. So we made our way there. I asked the engine driver if he was going to Kingston. He said he didn't know exactly, so I slipped half-a-crown into his hand and begged him to be the 11.15 to[6] Kingston. 'No one will ever know on this line what train you are or where[7] you are going.'

The driver hesitated for a moment.[8] Then 'All right,[9] gents,' he replied. 'Give me the half-crown.'

It was discovered[10] later on that the train we had taken was the Exeter mail,[11] that they had spent hours looking[12] for it, and that nobody knew what had become of it.[13]

J. K. Jerome, *Three Men in a Boat*

1 'the train of eleven fifteen.' 2 'from platform two.' 3 *entendre dire que.* 4 Tense? 5 § 54 (*b*). 6 *pour.* 7 *dans quelle direction.* 8 § 43. 9 *C'est entendu.* 10 avoid passive, § 17 (*b*). 11 *le train poste pour Exeter.* 12 § 76 (*a*). 13 § 119.

XVII

George's Adventure (1)

George told[1] us that one winter's evening, in foggy weather,[2] his watch had stopped at a quarter past eight. Unfortunately he forgot to wind it up before he went to bed. When he woke up[3] next morning, he looked at it and found it was a quarter past eight. He jumped out of bed,[4] had[5] a cold bath, washed, shaved, and looked at his watch again. For some reason or other[6] it had begun to go again and was now pointing to twenty minutes to nine. George seized it and ran downstairs. In the sitting room everything was dark and silent. There was no fire, no breakfast. George thought it a great shame[7] and made up his mind to tell his landlady what he thought of her[8] when he came back[9] in the evening. He put on his overcoat, snatched up his umbrella and rushed to the door. To his great surprise it was locked and bolted. He opened it quickly and ran out.

J. K. Jerome, *Three Men in a Boat*

1 *raconter*. 2 § 100 (*a*). 3 § 36. 4 § 104. 5 *prendre*. 6 *pour une raison ou l'autre*. 7 'that it was shameful.' 8 *dire son fait à sa logeuse*. 9 Tense?

XVIII

George's Adventure (2)

After running a quarter of a mile he thought it rather strange[1] that all the shops were shut and that there was hardly anyone in the streets. Certainly[2] the weather was very dark that morning and there was a good deal of fog, but it seemed rather strange to[3] stop all business on that account.[4] At length he reached Holborn. He pulled out his watch and looked at it. It pointed to five minutes to nine. He went up to a policeman and asked him the time. The man eyed him suspiciously. 'If you listen, you will hear the clock strike.' George listened, and the clock struck three.[5] 'But it only struck three', said he. 'Well, what time do you expect it to[6] strike?' 'Why[7] nine, of course.' 'Look here,[8] young man,' said the policeman seriously, 'you take my advice and go home quietly and don't let's have any more of it.'[9]

J. K. JEROME, *Three Men in a Boat*

1 *trouver un peu étrange que*+subj. 2 *Certes.* 3 § 69 (*a*). 4 'for such a reason.' See *pareil*, § 17 (*e*). 5 'three o'clock struck.' 6 § 84. 7 *Mais.* 8 *Écoutez.* 9 *n'en faites pas d'autres.*

XIX

Innocence Abroad (1)

When one is motoring on the continent, it is often a good thing to[1] know the language of the country one is passing through. At other times[2] it is better to be completely ignorant of it.

On a lovely night in[3] Provence we were bowling peacefully along the road from Avignon, when suddenly a whistle rang out.

'What's that?' asked George.

'The police!' I replied.

I stopped the car, and we saw two gendarmes approaching us on bicycles. One of them, who was a brigadier, came up to us and said in French 'Your rear-light is out!' (I remembered then that it had flickered badly[4] on the previous evening and that we ought to have had[5] it put right.)

'It is a very serious matter',[6] said he, 'to be riding[7] at night without a rear-light.'

Then he took a note-book out of his pocket, moistened the point of his pencil and continued. 'Accordingly I must take your name and address.'[8]

The situation looked[9] pretty serious and I was just going to begin a speech in French, when George stopped me.

'Speak English', he said. *Punch*

1 it is a good thing to, *il est bon de*+inf. 2 *d'autres fois.* 3 What preposition? 4 *vaciller terriblement.* 5 § 60 (*c*). 6 *C'est très grave.* 7 ride, *rouler.* 8 *vous faire un procès.* 9 *L'affaire paraissait....*

XX

Innocence Abroad (2)

I addressed the brigadier.

'We have been on a motor trip[1] in the South,'[2] I said, looking him sternly in the face,[3] 'the weather has been splendid, and the roads, though straight,[4] are good. We think[5] the French scenery delightful.'

'Your policemen are wonderful',[6] added George.

'We are on our way to Paris', I went on, speaking in a clear and distinct voice. 'We expect to spend the week-end there.'

The brigadier opened his mouth and kept it open.

'After that,' said George, 'we are returning to London by way of[7] the Channel. If there were a tunnel, we should return that way.'[8]

There was[9] a pause.

'Soon', I said, 'we shall be back at home. In the place where we live, there is a large swimming-pool....'

It was enough.[10] The brigadier shut up his notebook and put it back in his pocket.

'You will have the repairs done as soon as possible, won't you?'[11] said he.

'My friend and I are very fond of diving. Sometimes we get up before breakfast....'

But the gendarmes were not interested in what we did before breakfast. They got on their bicycles again[12] and rode off into the night.

Punch

1 *faire une randonnée en auto.* 2 *le Midi.* 3 *le fixant d'un regard sévère.* 4 § 90 (*c*). 5 *trouver.* 6 policemen, *gendarmes*; wonderful, *épatant.* 7 *par voie de.* 8 'it is by that way (*par là*) that we should go back.' 9 § 43. 10 *C'en était assez.* 11 *n'est-ce pas?* 12 get on...again, *remonter*, bicycle, *le vélo.*

XXI

At the Post Office

Scene I

Miss A. (entering and going up to the wire grating). Will you get[1] me Syd. 203, please.

Lady Clerk. Syd. 203. (She makes[2] a note on a sheet of paper, then she takes up the receiver.) Hallo! Is that the exchange? (No answer.) Hallo! What? Number engaged? Why I haven't given you a number yet. I want[3] Syd. 203. (To Miss A.) You're through. (She replaces the receiver and signs to Miss A. to enter the telephone box.)

Three minutes later

L.C. (taking up the receiver and speaking through[4] to the telephone box). Your time's up. Ring off, please.

Miss A. I say,[5] you've cut me off in the middle of the conversation.

L.C. You only paid for[6] three minutes. You can be connected again for[7] another threepence.

Miss A. But the gentleman will have gone by now.

L.C. How do you expect me to know[8] that?

Miss A. I must send a wire. Give me a form, please.

L.C. By[9] the door.

Ronald Pertwee, *Postal Orders*

take up the receiver, *décrocher le récepteur*
replace the receiver, *accrocher le récepteur*
Exchange, *le central* number engaged, *Pas libre*
You're through, *Vous avez la communication*
telephone box, *la cabine téléphonique*
Your time's up, *Terminé* Ring off, *Raccrochez*
You can be connected again, *On peut rétablir la communication*

1 *donner.* 2 *prendre.* 3 *demander.* 4 *directement.* 5 *Dites donc.*
6 *pour* must be used here. 7 'If you give again (*de nouveau*) six sous.'
8 § 84. 9 *près de.*

XXII

At the Post Office

Scene II

Miss A. (tearing down a telegraph form). Has anyone got[1] a pencil?

L.C. You can take mine, if you return it to me.

Miss A. Thanks...(handing in wire). There you are.[2] I hope that's all right.[3]

L.C. (turning over the form). Your name and address on the other side,[4] please.

Miss A. Oh, give it me. I'll write it.

L.C. I really must ask you[5] to be quick. The office is just closing.[6]

Miss A. There.[7] I've written my name and address.

A clock strikes one[8]

L.C. I'm very sorry. I can't take[9] this wire. It's after closing time.[10] I should like to oblige you, but they[11] are very strict about closing hours here.

Miss A. But it's only two minutes to.[12]

L.C. Oh, but we must go by[13] this clock.

Miss A. But what am I to do?[14]

L.C. Couldn't say at all.[15]

Ronald Pertwee, *Postal Orders*

1 § 17 (*c*) ('anyone' is feminine). 2 *Voilà.* 3 *ça va bien.* 4 *au verso.* 5 'I am obliged to ask you.' 6 'is going to close.' 7 *Voilà.* 8 'one o'clock strikes at the clock.' 9 *accepter.* 10 'the hour of closing is past.' 11 *on.* 12 two minutes to, *moins deux.* 13 go by, *se régler à.* 14 § 82. 15 *je n'en ai pas idée.*

XXIII

At the Post Office

Scene III

Miss A. You said there is delivery at Sydley tonight.

L.C. (taking down her hat from[1] a peg). Collection from here at 1.5, delivery at Sydley at 8.15.

Miss A. That will just do.[2] Give me a three halfpenny stamp[3] and I'll post the thing.[4]

L.C. Next counter.[5]

Miss A. (to 2nd Lady Clerk, who is in the act of[6] putting back the stamps in the safe). A three halfpenny stamp, that's all I ask, a three halfpenny stamp.

2nd L.C. The office is closed. I can't serve you with stamps[7] till[8] Monday.

Miss A. (to 1st Lady Clerk). For twenty minutes I have been[9] in this office, twenty intolerable useless minutes, and you drive me away empty-handed.

1st L.C. Customers are not allowed to[10] remain in the office after closing time. You wouldn't wish to get us into trouble,[11] I'm sure. (Shuts window and pulls down blind.)

Miss A. Oh, yes,[12] I would,[13] if only I knew how. At any rate,[14] there's one thing I've learnt today. I know now why they[15] put you behind a wire grating.

Roland Pertwee, *Postal Orders*

1 take down from, *décrocher à*. 2 *ça fera mon affaire*. 3 'a stamp of three sous.' 4 post, *mettre à la boîte*; the thing, *ça*. 5 *au guichet à côté*. 6 *en train de*+inf. 7 'I can't give you any stamps.' 8 *avant*. 9 § 37 (*a*). 10 § 71 (*b*). 11 *nous attirer des désagréments* 12 *Mais si*. 13 *je le voudrais bien*. 14 *du moins*. 15 *on*.

XXIV

A Voice in the Dark (1)

I was spending the week-end in an old country-house. Some of us[1] had managed to[2] get down[3] on Friday evening, but our host was still absent. He had been in France, my neighbour at dinner[4] told me,[5] and he intended to fly back to England[6] in the course of the afternoon and to reach home in the evening. At this moment the lady who was sitting on my right touched my arm, and asked me if I was afraid of ghosts. I assured her that far from[7] being afraid of them, I was particularly anxious to meet one.[8] 'Do you think I shall see any here?' I asked. 'You are almost sure to hear noises',[9] was the reply.

We were all tired out after a stifling week in London, so everyone went to bed early. While I was undressing, I heard the sound of a car on the gravel outside and I guessed that my host had arrived. I was in the act of getting into bed, when I was startled by a hoarse cough[10] in the opposite corner of the room. I sat up in my bed, wondering what was going to happen.

Punch

1 § 98. 2 'had been able to.' 3 get down, *y arriver*. 4 *voisine de table*. 5 Put 'told me' before 'my neighbour etc.' 6 'to return (*rentrer*) to England by air (*par la voie des airs*).' 7 § 81 (*a*). 8 § 8 (*b*). 9 *du bruit*. 10 'a hoarse cough...startled me.'

XXV

A Voice in the Dark (2)

'Good evening', came[1] a voice from[2] the corner. 'I'm so sorry to have missed you[3] this evening. We arrived at Croydon so late that I dined there, instead of coming straight home. I am delighted you were able[4] to come for the week-end. We were afraid you wouldn't be able[4] to get away, and, George, I can't tell you how happy I was,[5] when Ellen told me just now you'd left that dreadful animal behind.[6] Now I can look forward to a pleasant week-end. Breakfast from nine o'clock onwards[7] tomorrow morning, but I'm sure you'll be too tired to[8] come down before ten o'clock. Then we can discuss our plans. I'm all for[9] a game of golf in the morning and then we might go and see the match in the afternoon. Now I'm sure you must be very sleepy, so good-night, and let's hope it will be fine tomorrow.'

I switched on the light, but my host had nothing further to say from[10] the little loud-speaker in the corner.[11]

Punch

1 *me dit.* 2 'coming from.' 3 'not to have seen you.' 4 Mood? 5 Order of words? 6 For 'leave behind' say 'come without'. 7 from...onwards, *à partir de.* 8 § 81 (*b*). 9 *je penche pour.* 10 *par.* 11 *placé dans le coin.*

XXVI

Iseult to Guinevere

Use 2nd Person Singular (*tu*, *te*, etc.) throughout

Darling Guinevere,[1]

Thank you so much[2] for your very kind letter. I am afraid that after all I shall not be able[3] to be present at the Jousts. It is most[4] tiresome. I have not been at all well lately[5] and the doctors say I must have[6] a change of air, so I am ordered to[7] the French coast. The King has some cousins there[8] who live in a charming little house on the coast of Normandy.[9] I am starting tomorrow and I shall probably stay there during the whole month of May. It is too tiresome to miss[10] the Jousts and you cannot imagine how disappointed I am.[11] I hear that Sir Lancelot of the Lake is not going to compete this year for the Diamond on account of his health. I am so sorry.[12] People here[13] say he is afraid of being beaten and that there is a new Knight called Laverack who is better than anyone else.[14] Isn't it absurd? People here are so spiteful. How you must miss[15] the dear King! And you must feel very lonely at Camelot without any of the Knights.

Your loving,

Iseult of Cornwall.[16]

MAURICE BARING, *Dead Letters*

1 *Guenièvre.* 2 *infiniment.* 3 Mood? § 65. 4 *fort.* 5 § 13 (*a*). 6 I must have, *il me faut.* 7 Say 'to go to (*sur*)'. 8 *là-bas.* 9 'on the Norman coast.' 10 'not to be able to go to.' 11 § 107. 12 'I regret it very much (*fort*).' 13 § 113 (*b*). 14 'stronger than all the others.' 15 § 120. 16 *Cornouailles.*

XXVII

So Punch hurried out of the house and down[1] the street until he met the policeman.

'Officer! Officer!'[2] he cried, 'have you seen a donkey?'

'Yes, Mr Punch, I have seen such a thing—often.'[3]

'Which way did it go?'

'Which one?'

'The one you saw', cried Punch.

'But I've seen several', said the policeman. 'I once saw a grey one[4] and another one with black spots.[5] I've seen ever so many at one time or another.'[6]

'But the one you saw this afternoon? What was he like?'[7]

'I didn't say I'd seen one this afternoon. You asked me if I'd seen a donkey and I said I had.'[8]

'You're a very silly policeman!' cried Punch angrily.

On hearing these words the policeman looked sternly at Punch and drew out a large notebook. 'I must[9] ask you for your name and your address?'

'What for?'

'For saying[10] rude things to the police.'

So Punch had to obey. But it was a long business because the policeman wrote very slowly and could not spell very well.[11]

S. G. Hulme-Beaman, *Tales of Toytown*

1 'and went down.' 2 *Monsieur l'Agent.* 3 'it has often happened to me to see one' (§ 8 *b*). 4 *un gris* (§ 8 *b*). 5 *tacheté de noir.* 6 *tantôt une fois, tantôt une autre.* 7 *Comment était-il?* 8 I had, *que oui.* 9 *je suis dans l'obligation de.* 10 For construction see § 81 (*c*). 11 *ne savait pas bien l'orthographe.*

XXVIII

The Accusative Case

Use 2nd Person Singular except in the last sentence

Pamela was sitting in the car.

'You haven't forgotten your passport, as you did[1] last year?' I enquired.

'No, I haven't forgotten it. It's in the dressing case. I shall be able to get it out in a second,[2] when we go on board.'

I let in the clutch,[3] and away we went.[4]

On our arrival at Folkestone Pamela looked gloomily at the Channel.

'The sea is awfully rough. I would prefer to wait here till tomorrow, and I may as well tell[5] you that I haven't got my passport?'

'But you said....'

'I didn't forget the passport. I merely forgot the dressing case—which[6] is not at all the same thing. I'll go and book a room at the hotel. You ring up Emily and tell her to bring the dressing case by train tomorrow. When you've done that we'll go and have a bathe.'

I got through to Emily, who said she had noticed the dressing case in the hall. She also said she had noticed my own passport on the hall table.

'In that case,' said I, 'Bring back mine too, while you're there.' Which she did.

Punch

1 'as you did it.' 2 *en un instant.* 3 *embrayer.* 4 *nous voilà partis.* 5 *je dois t'avouer.* 6 § 16 (*d*).

XXIX

The Mayor's Breakfast (1)

The Mayor of Toytown had just finished his breakfast. The Inventor had sent him some excellent sausages and as soon as he had eaten them all, he rang for his secretary and commanded him to convey his thanks to the sender. While he was speaking, a noise was heard[1] outside, and, without even waiting to[2] knock at the door, Larry the Lamb rushed into the room.[3] He was a pitiable sight.[4] Tears were streaming down[5] his cheeks, and he was so overcome that for a few minutes he could do nothing but sob.[6]

'Why, goodness me,[7] my poor Lamb, what is the matter? What ails you?'

'Ba-a-ah',[8] sobbed the Lamb.

'Come, come',[9] said the Mayor. 'Pull yourself together and tell us what is the matter. Haven't you a handkerchief? There, there.'[10]

'Oh, Mr Mayor, sir,[11] have you had breakfast[12] yet?'

'Why, certainly I have had breakfast, I have eaten some excellent sausages, which the Inventor has sent me.'

S. G. Hulme-Beaman, *The Toytown Mystery*

1 *se faire entendre.* 2 Say 'without even taking the time to'. 3 *la pièce.* 4 *il faisait pitié à voir.* 5 *sur.* 6 § 6 (*f*). 7 *Mais, mon Dieu!* 8 *Bê...e.* 9 *Allons, allons.* 10 *Voilà, voilà.* 11 *Monsieur le Maire.* 12 have breakfast, *déjeuner* (verb).

XXX

The Mayor's Breakfast (2)

At the word 'sausages' Larry burst into tears again.[1] Neither the Mayor nor his secretary could console him. In the middle of this confusion, Ernest the policeman entered the room.

'Oh, good morning, officer,'[2] said the Mayor. 'Can you do anything to console this lamb? He seems to be too overcome to speak. I had[3] no sooner said that I had eaten sausages for my breakfast than he burst into sobs.'

'Oh, Mr Mayor, sir,[4] you've eaten my friend Dennis',* said Larry, and he sobbed in a heart-breaking manner.[5]

The Mayor and the policeman turned pale and glanced at one another, and the Mayor looked very uncomfortable.

'And I was just[6] saying what excellent sausages they were',[7] he whispered.

'But I don't understand', said Ernest. 'Do you mean that your friend got mixed up with the sausage machine?'

'Oh, yes, sir. We think he fell in.'

'Come, come',[8] said the Mayor. 'Perhaps things are not as bad[9] as you think. Try and tell us what happened.'

S. G. HULME-BEAMAN, *The Toytown Mystery*

* Dennis the Dachshund.

1 *à nouveau.* 2 *Monsieur l'Agent.* 3 Tense? § 44. 4 *Monsieur le Maire.* 5 *à fendre le cœur.* 6 just, *en train de*+inf. 7 *c'étaient.* 8 *Allons, allons!* 9 *grave.*

XXXI

The New Railway (1)

The Mayor was sitting in his study at the Town Hall, when the boy arrived. When he was told that the Inventor's assistant was asking to see him, he hastily put away a paper covered with noughts and crosses[1] and ordered the boy to be brought to him.[2] On hearing that the engine was finished, the Mayor immediately went to see the Inventor.

'That's[3] a fine sort of engine', said he. 'Will it work?'

'Why not?' asked the Inventor. 'It has a good big spring, and if the spring doesn't work, one can use the sail.* If it isn't windy enough to[4] use the sail one can always get out and push. Everything will be ready in a week. Meanwhile, don't forget that we want an engine driver.'

'Ah, yes, of course', said the Mayor thoughtfully. 'We will arrange all that. Is it very difficult to drive an engine?'

'Not at all', replied the Inventor. 'When you have wound up the spring, the engine will start. All you have to[5] to is to sit behind.'

'That doesn't sound[6] very difficult', said the Mayor.

S. G. Hulme-Beaman, *Tales of Toytown*

* Note. The engine was provided with a sail, in case the clockwork broke down.

1 *ronds et croix.* 2 § 87. 3 *Voilà.* 4 § 81 (*b*). 5 § 77. 6 *n'a pas l'air.*

XXXII

The New Railway (2)

On his return to the Town Hall the Mayor sent for Ernest the policeman, for he was determined that everything should go off smoothly[1] on the day of the opening of the railway line.

'Constable', he said, 'I have arranged for the new railway line to be open to the public today week, let us say, at three o'clock. No doubt there will be[2] a crowd, and I want everything to go off nicely.[3] We will have the band. I shall make a speech and then I shall open the line by driving a train myself[4] along the track for the first time.'

'You will have a nice ride', said Ernest. 'I only hope it will be fine.'[5]

'Give the order to the Town Crier to go round the town with a drum, so that everyone in Toytown may know about the ceremony.'

'Is the crier to[6] announce that you will make a speech?' asked Ernest. 'Perhaps it would be better to say so, because in that case we should not have a[7] crowd.'

The Mayor looked very sternly at the policeman.

'You are very stupid', said he. 'Your remarks don't make sense.'[8]

S. G. HULME-BEAMAN, *Tales of Toytown*

1 *aller bien.* 2 § 92. 3 *aller pour le mieux.* 4 'by driving myself a train etc. 5 § 90 (*f*). 6 *devoir.* 7 Omit 'a'. 8 *ne tiennent pas debout.*

XXXIII

The New Railway (3)

At last the great day arrived, the day on which the railway line between Toytown and Arkville was to be opened.[1] The sun was shining and the whole town was decked with flags; everyone had put on his Sunday best[2] and very early in the day the crowd had gathered in the field outside the town gate, where the train stood[3] on its shining rails. It was very much[4] admired and had it not been for[5] the soldiers posted all round, there is no doubt that the people would have got up on the engine and started it going.

Punctually at three o'clock the Mayor's coach[6] rolled up,[7] followed closely by Ernest the Policeman, looking very hot and out of breath.[8] The Mayor mounted the platform, while the band played as loudly as it could. The crowd cheered and the Mayor made his speech, but he spoke so long[9] that the people became tired before he had finished and they made so much noise that at last he had to stop, although he had still a good deal to say.

S. G. Hulme-Beaman, *Tales of Toytown*

1 open, *inaugurer*. 2 put on one's Sunday best, *s'endimancher* or *mettre son bel habit du dimanche*. 3 stood, *attendait*. 4 very much, *très*. 5 had it not been for, *sans*. 6 *le carrosse*. 7 Say 'arrived'. 8 Say 'obviously (*visiblement*) overwhelmed with heat and quite out of breath (*tout essoufflé*)'. 9 *longuement*.

XXXIV

Use 2nd Person Singular throughout.

Here is the King of Paflagonia seated at table, having[1] his breakfast with his wife[2] and his daughter Angelica. He is reading aloud a letter telling him of[3] the early arrival of his nephew, Prince Bulbo. He is so much absorbed in reading it[4] that he has let his egg get cold.

'What?' says Angelica, 'that brave Prince Bulbo, so handsome, so accomplished, so witty?'

'Who told you so?'[5] asks the King.

'A little bird',[6] says Angelica.

'Poor Giglio?'[7] says Mamma,[8] pouring out the tea.

'I wish,' growls the King, 'I wish Giglio would go[9]....'

'Would go on better?' says the Queen. 'Yes, dear,[10] he is going on better. Belsinda told me so this morning when she brought me my tea.'

'You are always drinking[11] tea', says the King with a scowl.

'That's better than drinking[12] brandy', replies her Majesty.[13]

'Well, well,[14] my dear, I only said you were fond of drinking tea', says the King, making an effort to[15] control his bad temper.

THACKERAY, *The Rose and the Ring*

Paflagonia = *Paphlagonie*. Angelica = *Angélique*.

1 *en train de* + inf. 2 *son épouse*. 3 'announcing to him.' 4 *par sa lecture*. 5 so, *ça*. 6 *mon petit doigt*. 7 § 13 (*b*). 8 *a maman*. 9 § 84. 10 *mon cher*. 11 § 76 (*a*). 12 § 57 Note. 13 *sa majesté la reine*. 14 *Allons, allons!* 15 *s'efforcer de*.

XXXV

The Woman in the Call-box

'She is certainly[1] taking rather a time.'[2]

'Rather a time!' said I. 'I should think she is![3] How long have you been waiting?'

He looked at the Post Office clock.

'Half-an-hour', he replied.

'There you are![4] I've been waiting nearly twenty minutes and she still goes on chattering.'

'You can[5] go in directly she's finished',[6] said he. 'I'm in no hurry.'

'Thanks very much. I wouldn't for anything[7] make you lose your turn. You've waited long enough for her to have finished[8] her conversation.'

'No matter. Please take my place!'

'Well, since[9] you insist. I certainly am in a great hurry. It is disgraceful that a post-office of this size[10] hasn't more call-boxes. Still,[11] even if it had, they would probably be full of chattering women!'

At that moment the woman opened the door of the call-box.

'At last!' I exclaimed, and strode rapidly towards it. However, instead of emerging, she merely[12] poked her head out of the door.

'John!' she called.

'Yes, dear', answered a small man, hurrying up to her.

'Two more pennies,[13] please.'[14]

Punch

1 § 79. 2 *tout son temps.* 3 *je vous crois.* 4 Say 'What did I tell you?' (imperf. of *dire*). 5 and 6 Tense? 7 *à aucun prix.* 8 § 90 (*a*). 9 § 31 (2). 10 *de cette importance.* 11 *D'ailleurs.* 12 § 6 (*f*). 13 *Encore quatre sous.* 14 2nd pers. sing.

XXXVI

A Modern Cinderella (1)

Use 2nd Person Singular throughout.

There was once a beautiful girl called Cinderella,[1] who lived in a large house in Park Lane with her mother, her two sisters and a crowd of servants. The two sisters of Cinderella were much older and plainer than she, and their mother had given up the hope of finding them a husband, but she took[2] Cinderella to dances[3] every evening.

One day when[4] she was in the middle of a delightful story,[5] her mother came in suddenly and cried,

'Cinderella, why aren't you resting, as I told you?[6] You know we are going to the ball this evening.'

'Oh, mother', pleaded Cinderella. 'Must I go to the ball?'

'Of course you must go.'

'But I have nothing to wear.'[7]

'I have told your maid to get a dress ready for you. Now go and rest. I want you to look your best[8] this evening, because I hear that that young Mr Hogbin is back from Australia.'

'Then may I come back, when midnight strikes?'

'You'll come back when I tell you.'

Cinderella made a face[9] and went upstairs to her room.

A. A. MILNE, *A Holiday Round*

1 *Cendrillon.* 2 *conduire.* 3 *au bal.* 4 § 11 (*b*). 5 Say 'absorbed by the reading of a charming tale'. 6 'as I have told it to you.' 7 *à me mettre.* 8 *être en beauté.* 9 *faire la moue.*

XXXVII

A Modern Cinderella (2)

Use 2nd Person Singular for the conversation between Cinderella and her mother, not otherwise.

Cinderella looked[1] very lovely, when she started for the ball, but her mother was not quite satisfied.

'Cinderella, I told you to put on the silver slippers.'

'Oh, mother,[2] they're so tight.'

'What nonsense! Go and put them on at once.'

The ball was in full swing[3] when Cinderella arrived. After several dances Mr Hogbin took her in to supper.[4] People[5] noticed that she looked much happier, when she sat down.

When supper was over,[6] she was about to[7] return to the ball-room, when a look of dismay came over[8] her face.

'Is there anything wrong?'[9] asked her partner.

'N-no', replied Cinderella, but she made no effort to get up.

'Well, shall we[10] go back to the ball-room?'

'Y-yes.'

She waited a moment, dropped her fan under the table, picked it up, and went out of the supper-room.

'Let's sit here', said she, when they reached the hall.[11] 'Don't let's go upstairs....If you see mother, I wish you'd bring her to me.'

A. A. MILNE, *A Holiday Round*

1 Translate 'looked' by *était*. 2 *maman*. 3 *battre son plein*. 4 *conduire au buffet*. 5 *on*. 6 § 35. 7 'was going to.' 8 *envahir*. 9 wrong, *qui ne va pas*. 10 § 84. 11 *le vestibule*.

XXXVIII

A Modern Cinderella (3)

Use 2nd Person Singular throughout.

Her mother came up[1] eagerly.

'Well, dear?'[2] she said.

'Mother, do take me home[3] at once. Something extraordinary has happened.'[4]

'A proposal from Mr Hogbin! I knew it. Is my little girl going to be happy?'

'I don't know', said Cinderella anxiously. 'There's just a chance.'[5]

The chance must have[6] come off, for, once in the carriage, Cinderella gave[7] a sigh of relief.

'You'll never guess what's the matter', said she laughing. 'Just try.'[8]

'I guess my little daughter is going to run away from me',[9] said her mother archly. 'Am I right?'

'That's the last thing I can[10] do. Just look at that',[11] and she stretched out her foot, clothed only in a pale blue stocking. 'I told you my shoes were too tight. I simply had to[12] kick them off at supper, and I only got one back. I wonder what they will do with[13] the slipper, when they find[14] it.'

A. A. Milne, *A Holiday Round*

1 *arriver*. 2 *ma chérie*. 3 *reconduire*. 4 'there has happened (*se passer*) something extraordinary.' 5 *il y a une chance*. 6 § 54 (*f*). 7 *pousser*. 8 'Try then (*donc*).' 9 *se sauver de la maison*. 10 Mood? 11 *Regarde-moi ça*. 12 *il a fallu absolument que*. 13 *de*. 14 *retrouver*.

XXXIX

The White Rabbit

Alice was beginning to get very tired of sitting[1] on the bank by the side of her sister and of having nothing to do. Once or twice she had peeped into the book her sister was reading, but it had no pictures or conversation in it.[2] 'And what is the use of a book,' thought Alice, 'without pictures or conversation?'

She was considering[3] whether it was worth while getting up and picking daisies to make a daisy chain, when suddenly a White Rabbit with[4] pink eyes ran close by her.[5]

There was nothing very remarkable about[6] that, and she did not think it very strange to[7] hear the Rabbit say to itself[8] 'Oh dear, oh dear! I shall be late.' But when the Rabbit took a watch out of its waistcoat pocket and looked at it,[9] she started to her feet, and after running across a field she had just time to[10] see it pop down a large rabbit hole under the hedge.

LEWIS CARROLL, *Alice in Wonderland*

1 'of remaining seated.' 2 Omit 'in it'. 3 *se demander*. 4 § 95 (*c*). 5 'passed quite close to her running (*en courant*).' 6 *à*. 7 § 69 (*a*). 8 *se dire à lui-même*. 9 'to look at it.' 10 *avoir juste le temps de*.

XL

Alice falls down the Well

Alice was not a bit hurt[1] and she got up again at once: she looked up, but it was all dark overhead;[2] before her was[3] another long passage and she could still see the White Rabbit hurrying down it. There was not a moment to be lost:[4] away went[5] Alice like the wind, and she arrived just in time to hear it say, as it turned the corner, 'Oh, my ears and whiskers,[6] how late it's getting!' She was close behind it[7] when she turned the corner, but the Rabbit was no longer to be seen:[8] she found herself in a long, low hall, lit up by a row of lamps hanging from the roof.

There were doors all round the hall, but they were all locked, and when Alice had been along[9] both sides, trying to open each door in turn, she walked sadly down the middle, wondering how she would ever manage to get out again.[10]

LEWIS CARROLL, *Alice in Wonderland*

1 *ne s'était pas fait de mal.* 2 'everything was dark above her head.' 3 *se trouvait.* 4 § 78. 5 Use *partir.* 6 Translate 'Oh, my ears and whiskers' by *Par mes moustaches.* Cf. the fable of La Fontaine in which the goat uses the expression *Par ma barbe.* 7 *juste sur ses talons.* 8 *visible.* 9 go along, *parcourir.* 10 Say 'get out of it'. Omit 'again'.

XLI

Alice leaves the Tea-party

This piece of rudeness was more than Alice could bear:[1] she got up in disgust[2] and walked away: the Dormouse fell asleep instantly, and the others took not the least notice of her departure, though she turned round once or twice, half hoping that they would call her back. The last time she saw them they were trying to put the Dormouse into the teapot.

'At any rate,[3] I'll never go there again', said Alice. 'It's the stupidest tea-party I've ever been at,[4] in[5] all my life.'

Just as she said this,[6] she noticed that one of the trees had a door leading right inside it.[7] 'That's very curious,'[8] she thought, 'but everything's curious today. I think I may as well[9] go in at once.' And in she went. Once more she found herself in the long hall and close to the little glass table.

'Now I'll manage[10] better this time', she said to herself, and began by taking the little golden key off[11] the table to unlock the door.

LEWIS CARROLL, *Alice in Wonderland*

1 § 7 (*a*). 2 'disgusted.' 3 *décidément.* 4 be at, *assister à.* Mood? 5 § 97 (*b*). 6 'As she was saying these words.' 7 *jusqu'à l'intérieur.* 8 § 16 (*e*). 9 *je ferais aussi bien de.* 10 *s'en tirer.* 11 What preposition?

XLII

The Looking-Glass Room

By this time she was up on[1] the mantelpiece, though she hardly knew[2] how she had managed[3] to get there. Already the glass[4] was beginning to melt, like[5] a silvery mist.

In another moment[6] Alice had jumped lightly down into the Looking-Glass room.[7] Her first care was to look whether there was any fire in the fire-place and she was quite[8] pleased to see that there was one,[9] which blazed as brightly as the one she had left behind.

'So[10] I shall be as warm here as in the other room, warmer, in fact,[11] because there will be no one here to scold me away from the fire.[12] Oh, how amusing it will be, when they[13] see me through the glass and[14] can't get at me.'

Then she began to look round her, and she noticed that the pictures hanging on the wall were all alive and that the very clock on the mantelpiece had the face of a little old man, who was grinning at her.[15]

LEWIS CARROLL, *Alice Through the Looking Glass*

1 'She was now perched on.' 2 *sans trop savoir.* 3 *pouvoir.* 4 *la glace.* 5 § 17 (*f*). 6 *L'instant d'après.* 7 *la salle derrière le miroir.* 8 *bien.* 9 *qu'il y en avait en effet.* 10 *Comme ça.* 11 *même.* 12 'to keep me away from the fire by (*en* + pres. part.) scolding me.' 13 *on.* 14 § 33. 15 *lui grimaçait un sourire.*

XLIII

A Portable Set

'Talking about[1] receiving sets,' said the Inventor, 'here is a set of a new kind, which I could sell you at a very favourable price.'

Ernest and the Mayor examined it curiously.

'It looks to me more like[2] a barrel organ', said Ernest.

'As a matter of fact,'[3] replied the Inventor, 'I have made[4] it in such a way[5] that one can use it as a[6] barrel organ, if one wants to. If you don't like the music broadcast by the wireless, you can hear other music merely by[7] turning the handle.'

'Excellent idea!' said the Mayor. 'But why is it mounted on wheels?'

'Well, if you don't like the Toytown broadcasts, you have only to[8] wheel it to Arkville, and when you are tired of the Arkville programmes, you will wheel it back to Toytown. It is what I call a portable set.'

'But wouldn't you have to[9] do a good deal of walking?'[10]

'Well, you can always harness a donkey to it. Then you will not only hear[11] the music, but you will have, at the same time, a nice ride.'

S. G. HULME-BEAMAN, *Wireless in Toytown*

1 *à propos de.* 2 *il m'a l'air plutôt de.* 3 *de fait.* 4 *fabriquer.* 5 *de telle façon.* 6 Repeat *de* (without the article) after *comme* (as). 7 § 47 (*f*). 8 § 77. 9 § 53 (*d*). 10 *beaucoup de marche.* 11 'not only you will hear.'

XLIV

A Land without Music

Mr Twiddler[1] has just bought a wireless set of the latest pattern.[2] While having tea with us the other day he explained all about it.[3] He appeared quite pained, when we told him we could only get[4] English stations.

'Ah,' said he, 'then you have never listened to[5] real music.'

A few days later he invited us to come round to his house[6] and listen to his set. 'The advantage of having a powerful set', said he, 'is that you hear something really good in the way of music. Tell me, how do you like[7] that?'

'It's very fine', said Ethel. 'Where does that come from?'

'From Berlin. You wouldn't hear music like that[8] in England.'

The music stopped and a voice spoke in German.

'What does he say?' asked Ethel, turning to me.

'I'm afraid I know[9] very little German', I replied.

As we were returning home, Ethel asked me why I had pretended not to understand German.

'To spare the feelings of our host.'

'Then what did the announcer[10] say?'

'He said, "You have just been listening to[11] a programme of English gramophone records".'[12]

Punch

1 *Monsieur Tourne-Manette.* 2 of the latest pattern, *dernier modèle.* 3 'he spoke of it to us at length (*longuement*).' 4 *avoir.* 5 *entendre.* 6 *passer chez lui.* 7 *trouver.* 8 *de la musique de ce genre.* 9 § 65. 10 *le speaker.* 11 See note 5. 12 *musique anglaise enregistrée.*

XLV

The Late Arrivals

Use 2nd Person Singular throughout.

Guest. My dear, I'm so sorry[1] we're late.

Hostess. What does it matter,[2] so long as you're here at last? I know exactly what happened. You lost the way.

Guest. Yes, you know what men are.[3] If only they'd condescend to ask the way! But of course they never do. Shall I leave the car here? Or will it be in your way?[4]

Hostess. Oh, leave it here by all means,[5] unless you'd rather[6] put it in the garage. It's over there. Drive right round the rhododendrons and turn sharp[7] to the left, no, wait a moment, I mean the right.[8]

Guest. Come along,[9] John, and do mind the grass. (They garage the car. John remains behind to attend to the car.) (To hostess) Oh, let's go in without waiting for John, you must be dying of hunger. I know lunch is ruined and your cook is sure to be[10] furious and give notice.

Hostess. What about John?[11]

Guest. Oh, don't let's wait for him. We're frightfully late already.

E. M. D. *Punch*

1 so sorry, *désolé que*+subj. 2 § 112. 3 § 16 (*c*). 4 *va-t-elle te gêner comme ça?* 5 'But certainly leave it here.' 6 'you prefer.' 7 sharp, *tout de suite.* 8 'it is to the right that I mean.' 9 *Viens donc.* 10 *va sûrement être.* 11 'And John?'

XLVI

An English Airwoman lands in Java

(An account by the natives.)

In a far-away kingdom lived a husband and his wife; they were immensely rich and they had an only daughter. They made her study[1] under the direction of most learned men,[2] so that[3] she became very learned. But when she came home, she did not understand[4] household affairs and was scolded by her mother. Finally she became angry herself, ran away and went and found a skilful plumber, and the two together made a machine with fire inside, to fly in the air.[5] In this machine she circled above her village, and finally landed there to the great astonishment of the people. Her parents, though still angry, were proud of her, and her father promised to forgive her, if she crossed the sea in her machine and came back safe and sound.

And so[6] she had to cross the sea, and arrived in the natives' own island, just as the fire inside the machine had gone out and she had to put in new fire.[7] And now she has still one more sea to cross, and, if she succeeds and comes home safe and sound her father will give her much money and build[8] her a house with a roof of corrugated iron.[9]

1 study, *faire des études*. For construction see § 60 (*b*). 2 *les plus grands savants*. 3 *si bien que*. 4 *ne rien entendre à*. 5 *dans les airs*. 6 *C'est ainsi que*. 7 new fire, *du nouveau*. 8 'will have built for her.' 9 *une toiture de tôle ondulée*.

XLVII

Driving Mother in the Car

Use *tu, te,* etc. throughout.

Mother. Here's a car coming,[1] John. I think you'd better slow down a little. It seems to me we are going rather fast. Look out,[2] keep your eyes on the road.[3]

John. All right, mother,[4] I know how to drive.

M. And don't forget to slow down at the cross-roads.

J. Don't worry. I won't forget. By-the-bye, shouldn't we have[5] taken the turning which we've just passed?[6]

M. Yes, I ought to have told[7] you. You'd better go on till you come to a place where the road is broader and then turn round...that's right.[8] Here's the turning, now we can go ahead. I think you'd better hoot here, there are a lot of children playing[9] in front of those little houses over there.... Now we shall have to hurry up, but don't forget the thirty mile limit.[10]

J. But we're not there yet.

M. We shall be there soon. Don't you think the engine's getting hot?

J. I don't think so.[11] Why?

M. There's a strong smell of burning.[12] It doesn't matter. We can have the engine examined, when we reach the hotel. Now, don't forget to look out for the traffic signals, when we get to the town.

E. M. D. *Punch*

1 'which arrives.' 2 *Fais attention.* 3 *ne quitte pas la route des yeux.* 4 *maman.* 5 § 53 (*b*). 6 *dépasser.* 7 *prévenir.* 8 *c'est ça.* 9 § 50. 10 *la zone de la vitesse limitée.* 11 § 29. 12 *ça sent nettement le brûlé.*

XLVIII

The farmer called his servants and asked whether they had seen in the fields any little creature that resembled[1] me. Then he laid me gently on the ground on all fours,[2] but I got up immediately and walked backwards and forwards to let those people see[3] that I had no intention of running away. They all sat down in a circle about me the better to observe my movements. I took off my hat and made a deep bow to the farmer. I fell on my knees, I lifted my hands and eyes and I uttered a few words as loud as I could.[4] Then I drew a purse from my pocket and presented it to him. He applied it close to his eyes, to see what it was, but could make nothing of it.[5] Thereupon I signed to him to put his open hand on the ground, I took the purse and poured out the gold coins into the palm of his hand. I saw him pick them up one by one and examine them, but he seemed to be wholly ignorant of what they were. He signed to me to put them back in my purse, and after offering them to him several times, I thought it was the best thing to do.[6]

SWIFT, *Gulliver's Travels*

1 § 94. 2 *à quatre pattes.* 3 *faire voir à.* 4 *le plus haut que je pus.* 5 *il n'y put rien comprendre.* 6 *ce qu'il y avait de mieux à faire.*

XLIX

At the Opera

Use 2nd Person Singular throughout.

A. What were you saying, my dear? That man on the stage is making such a dreadful noise.

B. Yes, isn't he?[1] Imitating[2] Caruso, I suppose. (Speaking louder) I was saying that my sister, Lady Robinson, has been laid up[3] at Cannes for six weeks with influenza.

A. Poor thing![4] That's the worst of Cannes.[5] Such a treacherous climate. She ought to try Cairo.

B. Isn't it very dusty there?

A. Oh, no. You[6] scarcely notice it in the hotels. Quite a number of smart people go there every year.

B. So they tell me.[7] Have you heard that the Duchess....

A. What did you say, dear? I didn't quite catch it.[8]

B. It's this orchestra making[9] so much noise. Really it's enough to drive you mad,[10] and so unnecessary. For example, why have drums?[11]

A. To please[12] the gallery, I suppose. Those people up there have no taste for good music. What were you saying about the Duchess?

B. We really can't talk in the middle of all this din. Wait till there's a solo.

KEBLE HOWARD, *London Voices*

1 *n'est-ce pas?* 2 'He is imitating.' 3 § 37 (*a*). 4 *La pauvre!* 5 *c'est ce qu'il y a de pis à Cannes.* 6 *on.* 7 'one has told me that.' 8 *je n'ai pas bien saisi.* 9 'which makes.' 10 § 80. 11 § 82. 12 *faire plaisir à.*

L

An Improbable Conversation

The other evening, just as I was going to sit down[1] to[2] dinner, the telephone rang. I unhooked the receiver and replied in a rather[3] grumpy voice. 'Is that[4] Welbeck 1234?' asked the telephone girl. 'Yes.' 'I have called you to ask (you) if you are quite satisfied with the telephone service.' 'What?' I replied in amazement. 'You are asking me whether I like the service?[5] Why,[6] I'm delighted with it.' 'Are you glad that the automatic system has been installed?'[7] 'Yes, it's a tremendous success, don't you think so? Such an improvement over the old system.' But the lady refused to allow herself to be drawn[8] into a discussion.[9] 'You are never given[7] a wrong number?' 'Oh, no, never.' 'Have you any complaints to make?' 'None whatever.[10] Thank you so much for having asked me.' 'You'll be sure to inform us if you have any?' 'Rather',[11] I replied, assuming an air of importance.[12] 'Don't forget to ring me up, if you have any observations to make.' I tried to prolong the conversation, but the telephone girl added nothing more, and I regretfully hung up the receiver.

Punch

1 *se mettre à table.* 2 *pour.* 3 *plutôt.* 4 *Est-ce bien....* 5 'if the service is to my taste.' 6 *Mais.* 7 Avoid passive. 8 *entraîner.* 9 *à discuter.* 10 'absolutely none (sing.).' 11 *Soyez tranquille.* 12 *faire l'important.*

LI

In a Tea-shop

Use 2nd Person Singular except when the waitress is being addressed.

Lady Nouveau. What a queer place![1]

Mme Riche. Isn't it odd? Such peculiar people![2]

Lady N. Shall we risk it? Or do you think we'd better find an hotel?

Mme R. We should probably be just as badly off[3] there. You know what these country hotels are.[4]

Lady N. Where shall we sit?

Mme R. What do you say to[5] that little table in the corner?

Lady N. But, my dear, there's no table-cloth.

Mme R. I suppose they don't have them in these places.[6] Perhaps it's just as well.[7] Here comes a waitress. What will you have?

Lady N. I wonder whether they have any China tea?

Mme R. I'll ask.[8] Do you keep China tea?

Waitress. No, madam, as a rule[9] our customers prefer the Cingalese variety.

Mme R. Oh, really!.... Well, please bring us some quite fresh[10] tea.

Waitress. We always make fresh tea[11] for each customer, madam.

Mme R. And some slices of bread and butter, cut very thin, and mind the butter is quite fresh.[12]

Waitress. We only use the best quality[13] butter, madam.

Mme R. I don't like that girl. I have a feeling[14] she's snubbing me.

KEBLE HOWARD, *London Voices*

1 § 3 (*f*). 2 'The people are so peculiar.' 3 *tout aussi mal.* 4 § 16 (*c*). 5 *de.* 6 'places of this kind (*genre*).' 7 just as well, *préférable.* 8 'I am going to ask.' 9 *d'une manière générale.* 10 quite fresh, *tout fraîchement infusé.* 11 fresh tea, *une nouvelle infusion.* 12 *très frais.* 13 *de première qualité.* 14 *j'ai l'impression que.*

LII

Watching the Sunrise (1)

After a long climb they arrived in the evening at the Hotel Rigi Kulm. As they were dead tired, they went to bed immediately after supper. Before going up to their rooms they had ascertained that a horn would be blown in the early morning[1] in order to warn travellers who wished to[2] get up to see the sun-rise.

They were not long in going to sleep and they remained sunk in slumber till a call on the horn awoke them. Then they jumped out of bed, wrapped themselves in blankets and made their way to[3] a wooden platform from which one had a magnificent view over the Alps.

'We are at least fifteen minutes late', said Harris in a vexed tone. 'The sun is above the horizon.'

'No matter,' said his friend, 'it's a magnificent spectacle.'

They were so absorbed in watching the sun that they did not notice a crowd which had gathered round the platform and was observing them with lively curiosity.

Presently Harris exclaimed, 'Why[4] the sun's going down!'

It was perfectly true. There had been two calls on the horn, one in the morning, the other in the evening. They had slept the clock round[5] and they were watching the sun-set.

MARK TWAIN, *A Tramp Abroad*

1 *de bon matin.* 2 who wished to, *désireux de*+inf. 3 *se diriger vers.* 4 *Mais.* 5 *faire le tour du cadran.*

LIII

Watching the Sunrise (2)

However the hornblower promised to make them hear his call the next morning, and he kept his word. Directly they heard the first blast on the horn they got up. It was dark and cold, and as they fumbled for the matches, they both felt sorry that the sun didn't rise in the middle of the day, when[1] it is warm and bright and[2] one isn't inclined to sleep.

They proceeded to dress by the light of two candles, but their hands shook so much[3] with cold[4] that they had difficulty in buttoning up their clothes. Suddenly Harris drew the curtain and exclaimed, 'Oh, what luck! We shan't have[5] to go outside after all. You can see[6] the mountains quite well from here.'

This good news cheered them up. Instead of going outside they sat by the window with lighted pipes and fell to[7] chatting. Gradually it got lighter[8] and the mountains began to stand out against the sky, but no sun appeared.[9]

'There's something wrong with[10] this sunrise', said Harris. 'What do you think about it?'

'I don't know', said his friend. 'There's a hitch somewhere[11]....'

'Why, I know what is the matter,'[12] went on Harris, 'we're looking at the place where the sun set last night.'

MARK TWAIN, *A Tramp Abroad*

1 *alors que.* 2 § 33. 3 *tellement.* 4 § 97 (*f*). 5 'we shall not have need to.' 6 'one sees.' 7 *se mettre à.* 8 *le jour venait.* 9 'the sun did not appear.' 10 wrong with, *détraqué dans.* 11 *il y a quelque chose qui cloche.* 12 *Ah, mais j'y suis.*

LIV

A Visit to the Seaside

Use 2nd Person Singular throughout.

A. So you're back in town! Did you have a good time[1] at the seaside?

B. Yes thanks, a glorious time.[2]

A. Wasn't the weather awful?

B. Well, yes. I suppose it must have been pretty bad, but I scarcely noticed it. That's the best of Westbourne.[3] There are so many things to do.

A. Yes, of course. Were there many people at Westbourne?

B. My dear, it was simply packed.[4] People who hadn't engaged a room beforehand couldn't get[5] one at any price.

A. How awfully jolly![6] I do hate a half-empty place, don't you?[7]

B. Simply loathe it![8] But there's no chance of[9] that happening at Westbourne. And the dresses! They alone were worth the journey.

A. There are some quite[10] nice shops at Westbourne, aren't there?

B. Yes, quite good. I used to spend most of the morning shopping,[11] and then in the afternoon there were the tea-shops. I went out sometimes in the evening, but not often. I preferred to remain in the hotel listening[11] to the orchestra, and watching the people.

A. Sounds splendid![12] And you're looking awfully well.[13]

B. Yes, the Westbourne air always does me so much good.

KEBLE HOWARD, *London Voices*

1 *s'amuser bien.* 2 Say 'gloriously (*follement*)'. 3 *C'est ce qu'il y a de mieux à W.* 4 simply packed, *bondé.* 5 *trouver.* 6 *Que ce devait être gai!* 7 *et vous?* 8 *J'en ai horreur.* 9 § 90 (*a*). 10 *assez.* 11 § 76 (*a*). 12 *Tout ça me paraît parfait.* 13 *avoir très bonne mine.*

LV

French Manners

Whenever I go to a tea party in France and[1] see the drawing room chairs arranged[2] in a precise circle[3] I cannot help remembering that this code of ceremonial manners is a legacy from the Grand Monarque and has hardly altered since....

There are many other forms of ceremonious politeness in France. A man kisses the hand of a married woman in greeting her, but not that of a girl. He raises his hat not only to greet a lady of his acquaintance on passing[4] her in the street, and that too[5] without waiting for her to[6] recognise him, but also to[7] a man. He never fails to raise his hat to[7] a woman, be she[8] princess or concierge.

Servants still address their mistresses in[9] the third person. They ask: 'When would Madame wish that I should bring her coffee?' They announce that 'Madame is served' when they mean that dinner is ready. Moreover these seventeenth-century locutions survive not merely in the houses of the old Aristocracy, but all over France and almost in every class. I remember hearing[10] the owner of a small café introduce the man to whom he had just sold his business[11] as 'one of our most charming[12] butchers.'

PHILIP CARR, *The French at Home*

1 § 33. 2 *disposer.* 3 *en cercle précis.* 4 *croiser.* 5 and that too, *et cela.* 6 § 88. 7 *pour.* 8 § 90 (*g*). 9 *à.* 10 § 58 (*b*). 11 *ses fonds de commerce.* 12 *sympathique* (before noun).

Section III

FREE COMPOSITION

(1) The art of writing Free Composition in French should be learnt from the study of French texts which you read in the course of your school work. Set vocabularies on given subjects may be learnt by heart from books, but the best general vocabulary is the one that you build up yourself from your own reading.

(2) A useful method is to procure an alphabetical notebook and note down words and phrases under each letter. These words and phrases may be divided into four columns, nouns, verbs, adjectives and adverbs. Whenever possible the noun and its appropriate adjective or the verb and its appropriate noun should be copied down together.

In some cases it may be found more convenient to employ the method used in the Special Vocabularies on pp. 123–135, and group the words dealing with a particular subject under a noun; for example, under the letter 'M' the words *la mer*, *la maison*, and *les mouvements* might serve as titles for grouping together words and phrases dealing with these subjects.

(3) You will often find that a good French-English dictionary, or a French dictionary like Larousse, is of more use than an English-French dictionary. *Le Petit Dictionnaire* by Dr Albrecht Reum (J. J. Webber, Leipzig) provides a storehouse of French phrases and idioms under each word, but the translation of the French is given in German.

(4) Try to get into the habit of thinking in French. If you frame your sentences in English and translate them into French, you will produce something that is neither French nor English.

(5) Before beginning an essay or narrative jot down in French the ideas which you intend to develop in each paragraph. Arrangement of material is of the greatest importance and every essay should have an introduction and a conclusion.

(6) *Ce qui n'est pas clair n'est pas français.* Sentences should be short and clear. Complicated sentences containing a number of relative clauses should be particularly avoided.

SPECIAL VOCABULARIES

Take place, happen, be (in a place)

il y avait une fois..., once upon a time there was...

Il était une fois un roi (in literary style), once upon a time there was a king

le mariage eut lieu, the marriage took place

la fête eut lieu, the fête took place

la réunion eut lieu, the meeting took place

un accident s'est produit, an accident has happened

il lui est arrivé un accident, he has met with an accident

Il lui est arrivé un malheur, he has met with a disaster

il y eut un grand fracas, there was a loud crash; a loud crash followed

il y eut un silence / ***il se fit un silence***, a silence ensued (or followed)

un bruit se fit entendre, a noise was heard

un incendie éclata, a fire broke out

il se trouvait être là, he happened to be there

il arriva que... / ***il se trouva que...***, it happened that...

il advint que..., it chanced or befell that...

je me trouvais alors à Paris, I was then in Paris

où se trouve la cathédrale? where is the cathedral?

dans cette rue se trouvait une vieille maison..., in this street was an old house...

cela s'est passé il y a dix ans, that happened ten years ago

comment cela s'est-il passé? how did that happen?

l'après-midi s'est bien passé, the afternoon went off well

la soirée s'est-elle bien passée? did the party go off well?

l'action de cette histoire se passe en France, the scene of this story is laid in France

Motion

approcher de } come or go near
s'approcher de } to, approach
aborder quelqu'un, come or go up to someone
accourir, run up, come running up (to, *vers*)
courir vers, run or rush up to
avancer } come or go forward,
s'avancer } advance
se diriger vers, make one's way to
se rendre à, betake oneself to, repair to
retourner, go back (*revenir*, come back)
se tourner vers, turn to (towards)

s'en aller, go away
partir (intr.), go, depart, leave, start
quitter (tr.), leave (a person or place)
se sauver, run away
s'éclipser } slip away, vanish
s'esquiver }
s'éloigner, move away
s'effacer, withdraw, stand aside
s'écarter, step aside, withdraw
se retourner, turn round
rebrousser chemin, retrace one's steps
aller au devant de quelqu'un, go to meet someone
aller attendre quelqu'un à la gare, go and meet someone at the station

passer devant une porte, pass a door
passer devant une maison, pass a house

passer par une ville, pass through or by a town
passer par une région, pass through a district

monter (tr. and intr.), bring or go or come up or upstairs
monter dans, get into (a car, bus or train)
grimper (intr.), climb up, clamber up

gravir (tr. rarely intr.), climb, e.g. *gravir une montagne*
descendre (tr. and intr.), bring or go or come down or downstairs
dégringoler, tumble down, come tumbling down

traverser, cross (e.g. *la rue*), pass through, get through (e.g. *la forêt*)
passer, cross, go over (a bridge or river)

parcourir, travel or ramble through (e.g. *la ville, les rues*), scour (e.g. *la campagne*)
parcourir une distance, cover a distance

Walking, Driving, Riding, etc.

se promener / *faire une promenade*, go for a walk, drive, ride, sail, etc.

faire une belle promenade, go for a lovely walk, drive, etc.

faire une promenade à pied, go for a walk

marcher, walk (as opposed to standing still or running)

se promener dans la rue, walk about the streets

faire une promenade à quelqu'un, take some one for a drive or ride or trip

revenir / *retourner* *à pied*, walk back

rentrer à pied, walk home

cheminer, tramp along, plod along

faire un petit tour, go for a short stroll

flâner, saunter

rôder (intr.), prowl

après deux heures de marche, after a two hours' walk

suivre un chemin, walk along a road

poursuivre son chemin, go on one's way

Distance

faire un bout de chemin, go a little way

faire un bon bout de chemin, go a good way

c'est un bon bout de chemin, it's a good way from here

faire deux milles à pied, walk two miles

faire deux milles en auto, drive two miles in a car

à mi-chemin, half-way

à mi-chemin de Londres, half-way to or from London

à mi-hauteur, half way up

à mi-côte, half way up the hill

Actions and postures of the human body

se lever, get up

se lever d'un bond, jump up

se tenir debout, stand

rester debout, remain standing

se redresser, get up again

se coucher, lie down

se mettre à genoux, kneel

s'appuyer sur, *contre*, lean on, against

se pencher en dehors, lean out

s'adosser au mur, lean one's back against the wall

se courber, bend, stoop

s'accroupir, crouch, squat

courir à toutes jambes, run as fast as possible

s'asseoir, sit down

je m'assis, I sat down (reflexive form implies action)

j'étais assis, I was sitting

assis, sitting
couché, lying
agenouillé, kneeling
appuyé, leaning (on, or against)
penché, leaning, stooping
adossé au mur, with one's back to the wall
courbé, bent, bowed, stooping
le dos courbé, with bent back
accroupi, crouching, squatting
marcher vite, walk quickly
tendre la main, hold out the hand
croiser les bras, fold the arms
serrer la main à quelqu'un, shake hands with someone
je lui ai serré la main, I shook hands with him

Sight

regarder, look at, watch
lever les yeux, look up
chercher des yeux, look about for
jeter un regard sur, cast a glance at
regarder fixement, stare at
baisser les yeux, look down
suivre des yeux, look after, gaze after
suivre du regard, gaze after
promener, porter ses regards sur, cast one's eyes over or towards
tourner ses regards vers, turn one's eyes towards
attacher ses regards sur, fasten one's eyes on
fixer quelqu'un, stare at someone
il promena ses regards autour de lui, he looked round him

La Ville

aller en ville, go to town
faire des emplettes, make some purchases
faire des courses, go out shopping (in a large town)
faire des commissions, do some shopping (e.g. buy the household provisions)
prendre la deuxième à gauche, take the second turning on the left
un arrêt de circulation, a traffic block
un parc pour autos / *un parc de stationnement*, car park
parquer une auto, park a car
une rue à sens unique, a one-way street
sens interdit, no entry
les signaux lumineux, traffic lights
les passages cloutés, pedestrian crossings
l'hôtel des postes, main post office
le bureau de poste, post office

Masc.	Fem.
l'hôtel de ville, town hall	*la place*, square
le théâtre, theatre	*la place du marché*, market place
le trottoir, pavement	*la bordure*, kerb
le magasin, shop	*la boutique*, small shop
le café, café	*la devanture*, shop front
le restaurant, restaurant	*la vitrine*, shop window
le garçon, waiter	*la serveuse*, waitress
le salon de thé, tea room	*la marchande des journaux*, woman at the bookstall
le kiosque, newspaper stall	*la papeterie*, stationer's shop
le bureau de tabac, tobacconist's shop (also sells stamps)	*la librairie*, bookshop
le taxi, taxi (*en taxi*, in a taxi, by taxi)	*la confiserie*, confectioner's shop
le chauffeur, driver (of taxi)	*l'épicerie*, grocer's shop
le receveur, conductor (of bus)	*l'auto*, *la voiture*, car
l'autobus, motor bus	*aller en auto à Paris*, to motor to Paris
aller en autobus, go by bus	

Adjectives to qualify 'la rue'

animé, lively
encombré, crowded
bondé de monde, thronged with people
bien éclairé, well lighted

La Campagne

à la campagne, in the country
en pleine campagne, in the open country
aller en villégiature, go for a holiday in the country
être en villégiature, be staying in the country
faire un pique-nique, go for a picnic
aller à la chasse, go hunting
aller à la pêche, go fishing.

Masc.	Fem.
le paysage, landscape, scenery	*la plaine*, plain
le bois, wood	*la forêt*, forest
le champ, field	*l'herbe*, grass

Masc.	Fem.
le chemin, road	*la route*,[1] (main) road
le sentier, path, lane	*la haie*, hedge
l'arbre, tree	*la feuille*, leaf
le talus,[2] bank	*la mousse*, moss
le village, village	*la chaumière*, (thatched) cottage
le ruisseau, stream, brook	*la rivière*, river
le pont, bridge	*l'eau*, water
le château, castle	*l'église*, church
le sommet, top	*la colline*, hill
le parc, park	*la prairie*, meadow
le lac, lake	*la montagne*,[3] mountain
l'étang, pond	*la mare*, pool
le berger, shepherd	*la bergère*, shepherdess
le mouton, sheep	*la vache*, cow
l'agneau, lamb	*la ferme*, farm
le troupeau, flock	*la charrette*, cart
le canard, duck	*l'oie*, goose
le fermier, farmer	*la fermière*, farmer's wife
le blé, corn	*la moisson*, harvest
le sillon, furrow	*la charrue*, plough
l'aubergiste, inn-keeper	*l'auberge*, inn

1 *au bord de la route*, by the roadside. 2 *un talus convert de mousse*, a mossy bank. 3 Note that *dans la montagne* often means 'in the hills' as opposed to 'in the plain'.

Les Vêtements

Masc.	Fem.
le chapeau, hat	*la casquette*, cap
le gant, glove	*une paire de gants*, pair of gloves
le pantalon, trousers	*la culotte*, breeches
le jupon, petticoat	*la jupe*, skirt
le veston, jacket, lounge-coat	*la blouse*, blouse
le gilet, waistcoat	*la chemise*, shirt
le complet, suit	*la robe*, dress
le smoking, dinner jacket	*la robe du soir*, (lady's) evening dress

Masc.	Fem.
le manteau, cloak	*la ceinture*, belt, waistband
le soulier, shoe	*la pantoufle*, slipper
les bas, stockings	*les chaussettes*, socks
les lacets, laces	*les chaussures*, footwear, shoes
le faux-col, collar (of shirt)	*la cravate*, tie
le collet, collar (of coat)	*la doublure*, lining
le collier, necklace	*la bague*, ring
le bouton, button	*la manche*, sleeve
le bouton de col, collar stud	
les boutons de manchette, cuff links	
le costume tailleur, tailor-made costume	
l'imperméable, mackintosh	
le pardessus, great-coat	

déchiré, torn	*serré*, tight
troué, in holes	*lâche*, loose
râpé, threadbare	*uni*, plain (of material or colour)
usé, worn	*rayé*, striped
en lambeaux, in tatters	

mettre, put on	*coiffé d'un chapeau*, wearing a hat
porter, wear	*ôter*, take off
s'habiller, dress	*passer*, slip on
se chausser, put on one's shoes	*se déshabiller*, undress
vêtu de, clothed in	*se changer*, change one's clothes
chaussé de souliers, wearing shoes	*habillé de*, dressed in

raccommoder, mend	*faire un point à*, put a stitch in, sew up
recoudre, sew on (a button)	*rapiécer*, patch
boutonner, button up	*doubler de* (*soie*), line with (silk)
déboutonner, unbutton	

Les Couleurs

De quelle couleur est-ce? What colour is it?

Variable adjectives

blanc, white
noir, black
bleu, blue
rouge, red
jaune, yellow
gris, grey
blanchâtre, whitish
noirâtre, blackish
bleuâtre, bluish
rougeâtre, reddish
jaunâtre, yellowish
grisâtre, greyish
rose, pink
violet (f. *violette*), violet
brun(e), dark, dark brown
mauve, mauve
pourpre, purple
châtain (masc. plur. *châtains* but rare in feminine), chestnut, auburn (of hair)

Invariable adjectives

marron, brown (of suit, dress or shoes)
bleu clair, light blue
bleu vif, bright blue
bleu marine, navy blue
bleu foncé, dark blue
bleu pâle, pale blue

Le Temps

Quel temps fait-il? What is the weather like?

il fait beau, it is fine, the weather is fine
nous avons un temps splendide, we are having magnificent weather
il fait du soleil, it is sunny
le soleil brille, the sun is shining
le ciel est sans nuages, the sky is cloudless
par une belle matinée de printemps, on a fine spring day
il fait chaud, it is warm
les grandes chaleurs, the hot weather season
une vague de chaleur, a heat-wave
le temps est à l'orage, there is thunder in the air
il fait frais, it is cool
la fraîcheur du soir, the cool of the evening

le temps se gâte, the weather is breaking up
le ciel se couvre, the sky (or it) is clouding over
le ciel se dégage, the sky is clearing
le temps s'éclaircit, the weather is clearing

il fait mauvais, the weather is bad (or wet)
le temps est instable, the weather is uncertain
nous avons un temps affreux, we are having dreadful weather
il fait du brouillard, it is foggy
il fait de la brume, it is misty
il ne fait que pleuvoir, it does nothing but rain
le temps est à la pluie, it is rainy weather
le temps est à la gelée, it is frosty weather
il fait froid, it is cold
il gèle dur (or *à fendre pierre*), it is freezing hard
il a gelé blanc, there has been a white frost
il neige, it is snowing
il fait de la neige, it is snowy weather
il fait frisquet ce matin, it's a bit chilly this morning

Les Sports

s'adonner aux sports, go in for sports
être passionné pour les sports, be very fond of sports
jouer au tennis, au football, etc., play tennis, football, etc.
faire une partie de tennis, play a game of tennis
faire une partie de canot, go on a boating trip
gagner la partie, win the game
s'inscrire pour un tournoi, go in for a tournament
un match va se jouer, a match is to be played

faire du tennis, go in for tennis
faire du football, go in for football
faire du cheval, go in for riding
faire de la bicyclette, go in for cycling
faire de l'auto, go in for motoring
faire du canotage, go in for boating

le joueur, la joueuse, player
le match, match
le terrain de football, football ground
l'arbitre, umpire
les spectateurs, spectators
l'équipe (f.), team
le terrain de golf, golf course
l'adversaire, opponent

le tennis, (1) tennis, (2) tennis court
le filet, tennis net
simple messieurs, gentlemen's singles
jouer un simple, play a single
faire des balles, have a knock-up
la balle, ball
la raquette, racket
double dames, ladies' doubles
double mixte, mixed doubles
la manche / *le set* } set

le ballon, ball (football)
la mêlée, scrum
marquer un but, kick a goal
réussir un but, kick a goal
dégager, clear (kick into touch)
passer, pass
le but, goal
la mi-temps, half-time
marquer un essai, score a try
transformer un essai, convert a try
dribbler, dribble
plaquer, tackle
les avants, forwards
l'ailier gauche, outside left
l'avant-centre, centre-forward
l'ailier droit, outside right
les demis, halves
les trois-quarts, three-quarters
les derrières, backs
le gardien de but, goal-keeper

jouer au golf, play golf
le trou, hole
le tertre de départ, teeing ground
la crosse, club
la pelouse (*d'arrivée*), (putting) green
la balle, ball (golf)
les sports d'hiver, winter sports
faire du ski, go skiing
faire du patinage, go skating
la luge, toboggan (in Switzerland)
luger, to toboggan

En Voyage

(par le train)

Masc.

le voyageur, passenger
le porteur, porter
le taxi, taxi (*en taxi*)
le billet, ticket
le guichet, ticket-office
le quai, platform
l'indicateur, time-table
le wagon, (railway) coach
le compartiment, compartment
le filet, rack
le coin fenêtre, window corner
le coin couloir, corner next the corridor
le marche-pied, footboard
le couloir, corridor
le wagon restaurant, restaurant car
premier service, first service

Fem.

la malle, trunk
la valise, suit-case
l'auto (*en auto*), car
la gare, station
la bibliothèque (*de la gare*), book-stall
l'affiche, the notice
la voiture, (railway) carriage
la place, seat (place in carriage)
la banquette, seat (wooden or upholstered)
la portière, door (of carriage)
une place de coin, corner seat
une place réservée, a reserved seat
la couchette, sleeping-berth
la veilleuse, night-light

retenir une place à l'avance, engage a seat beforehand
faire les malles, pack up one's things, do the packing
consulter l'horaire, consult the time-table
monter dans, get into (a train)
descendre de, get out of (a train)
baisser la glace, open the window
lever la glace, shut the window

la visite de la douane, customs examination
passer par la douane, get through the customs
la visite des grands bagages se fait à Paris, heavy luggage is examined at Paris
la visite des bagages à la main se fait à Dieppe, hand luggage is examined at Dieppe

manquer la correspondance pour Lyon, miss the connection for Lyons

le contrôleur, ticket collector
contrôler les billets, take or examine tickets

en tête, front part (of train)
en queue, back part (of train)
en voiture, s'il vous plaît, take your seats, please
vos billets, s'il vous plaît, tickets, please

ne pas se pencher en dehors, don't lean out
en cas de danger, tirer l'anneau, in case of danger pull the communication cord
tout le monde descend, all change here

(Sur le bateau)

s'embarquer, go on board
le pont, deck
à l'avant, in the bow
à l'arrière, in the stern
débarquer, disembark

faire viser son passeport, get one's passport visa-ed
la carte de débarquement, landing ticket
la passerelle, gangway

Au Bord de la Mer

Masc.

le sable, sand
les galets, shingle
le seau, bucket
le maillot, bathing costume
le transat, deck-chair
le parasol, beach parasol

Fem.

la plage, beach
la coquille, shell
la pelle, spade
la serviette, towel
la location, hire (of boat, bathing costume, etc.)

Masc.	Fem.
le canot, rowing boat	*la rame*, oar
le radeau, raft	*la périssoire*, canoe
le rocher, rock	*la jetée*, pier or jetty
le phare, lighthouse	*la vague*, wave
	l'algue, sea-weed

la marée monte, the tide is coming in
à marée haute, at high tide

la marée descend, the tide is going out
à marée basse, at low tide

se baigner, bathe
avoir pied, be in one's depth
savoir nager, know how to swim
faire la planche, float on one's back
l'eau est bonne, the water is warm

prendre un bain de soleil, sunbathe
prendre un bain, have a bathe
perdre pied, get out of one's depth
plonger, dive
faire un plongeon, take a dive

le pêcheur, fisherman
aller à la pêche, go fishing

faire la pêche à la crevette, go shrimping

profond, deep
peu profond, shallow
calme, calm
agité, choppy
démonté, very rough
moutonneux, flecked with foam

la mer est grosse, there is a heavy sea
la mer est mauvaise, the sea is rough
la mer est houleuse, there is a swell on
il fait un calme plat, there is a dead calm

Au Cinéma

le cinéma } the cinema
le ciné (colloquial) } the cinema
le fervent du cinéma, cinema fan
le film à cinq bandes, film in five reels
le film de reportage, news film

le film d'actualité, topical film
le bureau de location, booking office
les petites places, cheap seats
les places assises, sitting room
les places debout, standing room
la placeuse, seat attendant

le parterre, pit
la loge, box
le premier balcon, dress circle, grand circle
le deuxième balcon, upper circle
les fauteuils, stalls
la baignoire, ground-floor box

retenir une place, reserve a seat
la pièce fait salle comble, the play is drawing crowded houses
faire la queue, form up in a queue
la salle est bondée, the house is packed

la vedette de l'écran, film star
projeter une image sur l'écran, show a picture on the screen
présenter un roman à l'écran, show a novel on the screen
tourner un film, (1) take a film, (2) act in a film
tourner une scène, film a scene
faire du cinéma, act for the films

(1) SUJETS DE COMPOSITION

1. Ce que vous avez fait pendant les vacances.
2. Ce que vous comptez faire pendant les vacances.
3. Ce que vous pensez de la T.S.F. (Wireless)—les postes (stations) que vous écoutez et les programmes que vous préférez.
4. Décrivez une pièce que vous avez vue au théâtre ou un film que vous avez vu au cinéma.
5. Donnez vos impressions d'une grande ville que vous avez visitée.
6. Quelle saison de l'année préférez-vous—le printemps, l'été, l'automne, l'hiver? Donnez vos raisons pour cette préférence.
7. Écrivez une lettre à un jeune Français (une jeune Française) pour lui faire la description de votre école et de la vie que vous y menez.
8. Quelle est votre distraction (hobby) préférée?
9. Comparez les façons de voyager aujourd'hui avec celles d'il y a cent ans.
10. Une journée au bord de la mer.
11. Une description de Londres en l'an 2000.
12. Quel métier ou quelle profession considérez-vous comme rendant le plus de services à l'humanité?
13. L'influence des journaux.
14. Les sports obligatoires dans les écoles.
15. La journée d'un facteur (postman) de village.
16. Est-ce une perte de temps que de lire des romans?
17. 'En Angleterre on consacre trop de temps aux sports.' Critiquez cette opinion.
18. Où voudriez-vous vivre, en ville ou à la campagne?
19. Quel genre de film préférez-vous voir au cinéma?
20. Quel est votre romancier préféré? Faites le résumé d'un de ses ouvrages.
21. La traversée de l'Atlantique par la voie des airs.
22. Quel est le plus grand homme vivant? Expliquez les raisons de votre choix.
23. Quel pays étranger aimeriez-vous le mieux à visiter?

24. Décrivez la scène qui se passe dans une gare le jour du commencement des grandes vacances (summer holidays).
25. Les émissions radiophoniques font-elles du tort aux théâtres et aux concerts?
26. Quel est à votre avis le meilleur trimestre (term) de l'année et pourquoi?
27. Écrivez à un jeune Français (une jeune Française) pour lui proposer un échange de correspondance.
28. L'influence du cinéma est-elle bonne ou mauvaise?
29. Racontez la journée d'un agent de police (policeman).
30. On vous a donné un demi-congé (half-holiday) par une belle après-midi de juin. Dites comment vous allez le passer.
31. Quelle partie de la journée aimez-vous le mieux? Dites pourquoi.
32. Donnez les impressions d'un jeune Français qui visite Londres pour la première fois. (Écrivez à la première personne et employez le passé indéfini (parfait).)
33. Quel journal anglais préférez-vous? Donnez des raisons pour votre préférence.
34. On vous a offert de payer vos frais de séjour dans un pays étranger, y compris les dépenses du voyage. Quel pays allez-vous choisir et pourquoi?
35. À quelle profession vous destinez-vous? Expliquez les raisons de votre choix.
36. On a dit que les vêtements sont une indication du caractère. Quelle est votre opinion à ce sujet?
37. Établir (draw up) le programme d'une soirée de T.S.F., qui conviendrait le mieux à vos goûts. Donnez les raisons de vos préférences.
38. Quels sont, à votre avis, les meilleurs moyens d'éviter les accidents d'automobile?
39. Quels seront les avantages de la télévision? Seront-ils aussi grands que ceux de la radiophonie?
40. Croyez-vous que la radiophonie puisse servir à l'instruction dans les salles de classe?
41. Préférez-vous la vie d'un(e) externe (day boy or day girl) ou celle d'un(e) interne (boarder)?
42. Quel genre de lecture aimez-vous le mieux—aventures, histoire, voyages, romans, journaux, langues modernes?

43. Pourquoi n'y a-t-il pas de cafés en Angleterre, comme il y en a sur le continent?
44. Si vous avez un long parcours à faire, préférez-vous voyager en auto ou en chemin de fer?
45. Si on vous offrait l'occasion d'aller passer deux ou trois mois dans un des Dominions britanniques, lequel choisiriez-vous, et pourquoi?

(2) NARRATIVE

1. When the narrative is in the 1st person singular or plural, the Past Indefinite (perfect) should be used.

2. When the narrative is in the 3rd person, the Past Definite should be used.

3. (*a*) Il y avait, there was, is *descriptive* and refers to an *unlimited* period of time.

(*b*) Il y eut, there ensued, there followed, is a *narrative* tense and refers to one of a series of events *limited* in point of time.

e.g. Il y eut un silence   A silence ensued

Cf. Alors ce fut une explosion de rires
Then there was (i.e. followed) an explosion of laughter
Il comprit   He realised   Il sut   He learned or discovered
Il put   He succeeded in...

4. Temporal Clauses can often be replaced

(*a*) by prepositional phrases:

À mon retour	On my return
Avant son départ	Before he left
Après son départ	After he left
Dès son arrivée	As soon as he arrived
À mon reveil	When I woke up
Pendant leur entretien	While they were talking
Sur ces entrefaites	While this was going on

(*b*) By participles referring to the subject of the sentence:

Aussitôt arrivés nous avons pris le thé
As soon as we arrived, we had tea

5. Liveliness may be introduced

(*a*) by the use of the Present tense to denote actions rapidly following one another, e.g.

On arrive à la maison, on enfonce la porte, on entre, on arrête le voleur (*b*) by the use of *voilà* and the past participle, e.g.

Encore quelques minutes et les voilà partis
A few minutes more and they were off

(*c*) by the occasional use of the 'Historic' Infinitive, e.g.

Et tout le monde de rire
And everyone laughed

6. When the words 'he said', 'he replied' and similar expressions occur between sentences in inverted commas, the inverted forms *dit-il* and *répondit-il* must be used.

CANEVAS À DÉVELOPPER

1

Voyage en aéroplane dans un pays inconnu

Circonstances du départ—la route—léger accident à mi-chemin—descentes—réparations—arrivée des sauvages—leur attitude—nouveau départ—fin du voyage.

(Cambridge Local School Certificate, December 1927)

2

Rêve d'écolier (A schoolboy's dream)

Jean se prépare à faire ses devoirs—paresseux, il s'endort—il entend ses livres qui commencent à parler—ce qu'ils disent—la porte s'ouvre—son père arrive.

(Cambridge Local School Certificate, December 1929)

3

Un voyage en chemin de fer—le départ—les personnes que vous rencontrez dans le train—ce que vous voyez par la fenêtre—l'arrivée—les amis qui vous accueillent.

(Cambridge Local Junior, July 1932)

4

Scouts in Camp

Éclaireurs—camp—description—nuit—voleurs—alarme—courage des jeunes gens—détails—résultat.

(Cambridge Local School Certificate, December 1932)

5

Fidelité d'un chien

Musicien malade—hôpital—vend chien à dame riche—plus tard—salon—fenêtre ouverte—musique dans la rue—résultat.

(Cambridge Local School Certificate, July 1932

6

The lost ring recovered

Dame en bateau—bague tombe à l'eau—amis vont pêcher—rapportent poissons—cuisinière les prépare pour souper—bague retrouvée—où?

(Cambridge Local School Certificate, December 1935)

7

The parrot and the burglar

Perroquet—acheté par enfants—apprend à parler—nuit—cambrioleurs—perroquet réveillé—alarme—résultat.

(Cambridge Local School Certificate, December 1936)

8

Le prix des œufs

Georges I, de passage en Hollande—descend à une auberge—demande des œufs—on les lui apporte—on lui présente la note—200 francs—'Pourquoi les œufs sont-ils si chers en Hollande?'—réponse de l'aubergiste—œufs abondants, rois rares.

9

Le corbeau et le renard

Un corbeau vole un morceau de fromage—perche sur un arbre—un renard s'approche—flatte le corbeau—loue sa belle voix—le corbeau ouvre le bec pour chanter—laisse tomber le fromage—le renard le saisit—morale.

10

Le cuvier (the wash-tub)

Jacquinot bon mari, mais faible—sa femme l'oblige à faire le ménage—lui donne une liste de choses à faire (laver le linge, faire la cuisine, soigner le bébé)—un jour elle tombe dans le cuvier—supplie son marie de l'en tirer—réponse—'Ceci n'est pas sur ma liste'—la femme promet d'obéir à son mari—joie de Jacquinot—il déchire la liste.

11

Un ouvrier débrouillard (resourceful)

Un ouvrier creuse un puits—une partie du puits s'écroule—l'ouvrier ôte son chapeau et son veston—les pose par terre—se cache—des voisins s'approchent—ils croient que l'ouvrier est au fond du puits—ils enlèvent la terre écroulée—l'ouvrier sort de sa cachette—les remercie de leur aide et s'en va.

12

Vice Versa

Puissance magique d'un talisman—un père et un fils changent de place—le père prend l'aspect extérieur de son fils et le fils celui de son père—on envoie le père à l'école—incidents pénibles—se sauve et revient à la maison—talisman opère une seconde fois—le père et le fils reprennent leurs formes primitives.

13

Les honoraires du médecin

Un médecin avait guéri un petit enfant—la mère reconnaissante brode une bourse—l'offre au médecin—celui-ci la refuse—demande ses honoraires (fee)—Combien?—deux mille francs—la mère ouvre la bourse—en tire cinq billets de mille francs—en donne deux au médecin—se retire avec dignité.

14

L'erreur de l'évêque

Un évêque anglais aimait beaucoup les enfants—il décide de rendre visite à la famille d'un ami—sonne—entre—s'arrête devant la porte du salon—ôte son manteau—s'en couvre la tête—entre en rugissant comme un lion—cris d'alarme—l'évêque se découvre—voit deux vieilles dames—il s'était trompé de maison.

15

Défense de fumer

Réunion de gros commerçants (wealthy business men) dans un cercle—pancarte (placard) fixée à la porte—DÉFENSE DE FUMER—étonnement des commerçants—ils jettent cigares et cigarettes—un mendiant les ramasse—à l'intérieur personne ne sait rien de la pancarte—on l'arrache—d'où vient-elle?—le mendiant l'avait accrochée lui-même.

16

Trois amis voyagent en chemin de fer—un des trois s'endort—les deux autres lui prennent son billet—le voyageur endormi se réveille—ne retrouve plus son billet—on entend le contrôleur (ticket collector) qui s'approche—on conseille au voyageur de se cacher sous la banquette—le contrôleur arrive—on lui montre trois billets—où est le troisième voyageur?—'Il préfère voyager comme ça.'

17

Les grandes vacances—tout le monde part pour le bord de la mer—Madame A. et Madame B. se rencontrent dans un compartiment de chemin de fer—se reconnaissent avec surprise—dix ans depuis leur dernière rencontre—conversation—comment Madame A. a-t-elle reconnu Madame B.?—réponse—à son chapeau.

18

Un monsieur entre dans un bureau de poste—achète timbre—le laisse tomber sur le comptoir—le timbre commence à s'éloigner—surprise du monsieur—ne peut pas croire ses yeux—le timbre arrive au bout du comptoir—monte le mur—descend—arrive à portée de la main—solution du mystère—le timbre était tombé sur le dos d'une mouche.

19

Un fou inoffensif dans un asile d'indigents (workhouse)—le directeur va le conduire dans une maison d'aliénés (lunatic asylum)—loue une voiture—y fait monter le fou—celui-ci aperçoit l'ordre d'admission dans la poche du directeur—le saisit—on arrive à destination—le fou descend de voiture—dit qu'il a amené un fou—montre l'ordre d'admission—on enferme le directeur—le fou repart dans la voiture.

20

Les habitants de Hameln tourmentés par des multitudes de rats—les moyens qu'ils essaient pour s'en débarrasser—peine perdue—un homme se présente—s'offre à faire disparaître les rats moyennant une récompense—on accepte l'offre—l'homme joue de la flûte—les rats le suivent—il les conduit au bord d'une rivière où ils se noient—réclame sa récompense—on la lui refuse—il se remet à jouer—cette fois les enfants de la ville le suivent—il les conduit à une montagne—la terre s'ouvre—l'homme et les enfants y disparaissent.

(3) CONTINUATION EXERCISES

I

(Schulz tells his friend Kunz about a wire he has received announcing the arrival of the great musician Krafft.)

Translate into French:

After leaving his friend, Schulz went and asked the exact time of the train; then he called at the butcher's and the pastrycook's. At last he arrived home,[1] showed Salome the provisions which he had bought, and gave them to her for the next day's dinner. He went to bed at ten, but he was as excited as a child at Christmas, and remained awake the whole night.

He got up at half-past six, for he was afraid of missing the train. Happily, it was fine. Schulz dressed and went down to the cellar, wondering what wine he ought to choose in order to please the great musician....Salome did not succeed in making him drink a drop of coffee, for he assured her that Christopher would not have had his breakfast either.

At the station he discovered[2] that he had no hat and that he had arrived three-quarters of an hour too soon.[3] He went on to the platform, instead of waiting at the exit, and, after all, in the crowd that got out of the express, he did not see anybody who resembled[4] the portraits of Krafft.

1 § 96. 2 *s'apercevoir*. 3 *à l'avance*. 4 § 94.

Continue the above story:

Schulz returns home and hears from neighbours that the visitor came and found nobody at home. Disconsolate search; at last sees a man resting in a field, and loudly sings the first bars of one of the composer's songs; man starts up and greets him; visit successful after all.

(General School, Midsummer 1930)

II

(A landslide has taken place on a light railway serving a mine and Jacques is buried beneath a heap of sand and wooden beams.)

Translate into French:

Philippe turned towards the workmen. 'Have you tried to save the poor lad?' he asked. 'We have been working for[1] half-an-hour,' answered one of them, pointing to an enormous hole, 'but these beams may fall at any moment and we dare not continue.'

Taking off his hat and coat, Philippe knelt down near the hole and listened. There was no sound. 'Jacques,' he shouted, 'can you hear me?' A feeble voice answered, 'Ah, it's you, Monsieur Derblay; then I am saved. I can't move, and I believe I have a broken leg.'

'Don't be afraid, Jacques, we are going to pull you out of there.'

Philippe understood that the task would be difficult and dangerous. A few workmen would have to[2] enter[3] the hole and release the boy; the others would hold up the beams as much as possible.[4] And there was not a moment to lose.

to release, *dégager*. to hold up, *soutenir*.

1 § 37 (*a*). 2 'it was going to be necessary.' 3 *pénétrer dans*. 4 *de leur mieux*.

Continue the story using the following analysis:

Workmen protest it is too dangerous. Philippe enters alone and three men then follow him. Crowd silent and anxious. At last one man appears; then others with unconscious boy. Doctor arrives and pronounces his case not serious. Relief and gratitude of the mother.

(General School, December 1930)

III

Translate into French:

The Escape of the Marquis

The mistress of the inn hastened towards him and called her two daughters. They helped him to get down from his horse, and immediately he fainted. For a fortnight he had to stay in bed, where he was admirably cared for by his three hostesses. One evening he noticed that the mother looked troubled; soon afterwards, a German officer entered and began to talk[1] with her, using[2] a language which he did not understand. When he had gone, the marquis said to his hostess: 'That officer came to make me a prisoner, did he not?' 'Yes', she replied, with tears in her eyes. 'Well, there is some money in my pocket', he exclaimed. 'Buy me some peasant's clothes, and I will set off to-night.'

1 Say 'began a conversation' (*entamer une conversation*). 2 Say 'in a language'.

Continue the story by describing how the marquis disguises himself, tells a plausible tale to the soldier posted at the inn-door, eludes the guard at the frontier, and arrives safely in France.

(General School, December 1931)

IV

(The Narrator is seated at a café, watching the traffic go by. Suddenly he sees a crumpled letter thrown out of the window of a carriage. The traveller in the carriage puts his head out of the window, hesitates for a moment, then resumes his seat.)

Translate into French:

At this moment, a girl of about sixteen[1] who was crossing the street saw the little ball[2] of paper and picked it up. She read the letter and smiled. Then she looked at the café, consulted her purse, and finally came and sat at a table quite near the one which I was occupying.

Holding a newspaper in front of my face, I watched her with curiosity. When the waiter arrived she asked for a cup of chocolate, some ink, paper and a pen; then she began to copy the letter which she had found.

At the third line she hesitated and cast a timid glance towards me. Reassured, doubtless, on seeing[3] my grey beard, she said, 'Excuse me,

1 *dans les seize ans*. 2 *la boulette*. 3 *à la vue de*.

sir, but could you explain to me this word, which I do not understand?' She held out the letter to me, and I seized the opportunity of reading very rapidly the whole page.

Continue the above story, either drawing on your imagination or using the following outline:

The letter is from a lady, reproaching the gentleman for his neglect of her. On being asked how this could interest her, the girl explains that she has quarrelled with her sweetheart and that she is sure he will not be able to resist such eloquent and beautiful language.

(General School, June 1932)

V

Translate into French:

One day, the old man was working in his garden, with his dog, as usual, close by.[1] The weather was hot, and after working for some time, he threw down his spade and wiped his forehead. As he did so,[2] he noticed that the animal was scratching the earth at a spot a little way off.[3] There was nothing very strange in[4] this, as[5] all dogs are fond of scratching, and so he went on with his digging.[6] But then the dog ran up to his master, barking loudly, and ran back to the spot where he had been scratching. This he did several times, till the old man wondered what could be the matter.[7] Picking up his spade, he followed the dog to[8] the hole that the latter had just made.

1 'quite close to him.' 2 *sur ces entrefaites.* 3 *un peu éloigné.* 4 *à.* 5 *car.* 6 'continued to dig.' 7 § 112. 8 *jusqu'à.*

Write about 150 words in French based on the following outline, in continuation of the above narrative:

The old woman came out too, curious to know what was happening. The man began to dig, struck something solid, and drew out a box full of gold and silver coins. What the old couple did with the money.

(Matriculation, September 1929)

VI

Translate into French:

One night the wind was howling and the rain was beating against the windows. Beauchamp and I were sitting by the fire and smoking,[1] when the door suddenly opened and a girl came in.

She was so small that at first we thought she was a child. Her pale face was wet, for it was raining, her long fair hair hung over her shoulders, and she was laughing.

'May I come in?' she said.

We had both risen. 'Of course', said Beauchamp. She shut the door, approached the fire, and warmed her hands.

Beauchamp poured out a glass of wine.

'Drink that', he said.

She drank it and then laughed again like a happy child.

'Well,' said Beauchamp at last, rather severely,[2] 'who are you, and where do you come from, and why have you come?'

Then she began her story.

1 *en train de*+inf. 2 *d'un ton plutôt sévère.*

Write about 150 words in French, based on the following outline and *in the first person*, in continuation of the above narrative:

The girl was the daughter of a Frenchman who lived in London. A year ago she had returned from a school in Brussels. Her father had found her a post in a shop just before he died. A week ago she had lost her post, and was now without money. Beauchamp was a painter (*peintre*). Someone had told her that he wanted a model (*un modèle*) for a picture he was going to paint.

(Matriculation, June 1930)

VII

Translate into French:

Agnes, recognising Helen Sawrey, who occupied the neighbouring house, asked her in a whisper:

'Has my cook seen you? She is a spy.'

'Nobody has seen me.'

'God be praised for it[1].'

She took her into her bedroom, whither I followed them. She would have to[2] conceal Helen for several days or at least several hours till all those policemen were deceived[3] and tired out. I was asked to watch[4] the street and we hoped that, when I gave the signal, the unfortunate woman would be able to escape by the little garden gate.

She endeavoured to make us understand that she was being hunted down for having helped friends of the royalists to conspire against the State. The truth was quite[5] different: she was the victim of the vengeance of a local tradesman.

1 *en.* 2 'it was going to be necessary to.' 3 Avoid the passive by using *on.* 4 *surveiller.* 5 § 17 (*g*).

Continue the above narrative in French, limiting yourself to about 150 words. You may draw on your imagination or use the following outline:

Agnes lends Helen Sawrey some of her husband's clothing in which to disguise herself. Police arrive almost immediately. Helen, making her way over the roofs of the neighbouring houses, gets away by an outside stairway. Police threaten Agnes, who denies that Helen has been in her house.

(Matriculation, September 1930)

VIII

Translate into French:

'Citizeness,' the pretty girl said to her, 'tomorrow evening a man who loves you will be waiting at the corner with a carriage. Take this parcel; it contains clothes like[1] those I am wearing; during supper you will put them on in your bedroom. We resemble one another; in the twilight we might easily be taken one for the other. Gilles, the warder, will help us. With him descend the staircase (of which he carries a key) leading to my father's lodge. On that side of the prison the gate is neither locked nor guarded. Above all, avoid being seen by my father. Gilles will lean against the lodge window and say, as if he were talking to me: "Au revoir, Rose, and remember Gilles!"'

1 *pareil à.*

As Fanny listened, hope filled her heart. 'Why, dear child,' she said, 'are you ready to help in this way a woman whom you scarcely[2] know?'

2 *à peine.*

Write about 150 words in French in continuation of the above narrative. You may draw on your imagination or use the following outline:

Rose had been bribed by a friend of Fanny's and with the money she hoped that she and the gaoler would be able to marry. Fanny realised that Rose, if discovered, would be put to death, and refused the proffered help. Disappointment and entreaties of the girl.

(Matriculation, January 1931)

IX

Translate into French:

'Look out! there's danger', shouted one of the three men who were on the engine. Quickly looking,[1] the driver saw the red light, and at once applied his brakes.

The speed of the train, in which there were more than 200 passengers, became slower, and when at last the train stopped, the engine was close to brave little Jack's lantern.

The men sprang to the ground.

'What's the matter, boy,[2] why have you[3] dared to stop us in this way?' cried the driver, seizing his arm.

'Oh!' cried Jack, 'I had to[4] do it, or you would have gone into[5] the river; the rails are torn up on the bank yonder.'

'Come up on the engine, boy, with me.'

'Oh no!' the terrified boy replied. 'I should be killed if they knew I had warned you.'

With[6] these words he ran away into the woods just as a policeman, who had been travelling[7] in the train, approached.

1 *d'un regard rapide.* 2 *petit.* 3 2nd pers. sing. 4 *il a bien fallu que.* 5 'fallen into.' 6 *à.* 7 Imperfect.

Write a French Essay of about 150 words in continuation of the above. You may enlarge on the following outline or draw on your imagination:

Jack had overheard conversation of a band of criminals whom his drunken father had joined. Plan to wreck train and rob passengers. Police discovered everything. Criminals captured. Father pardoned for Jack's sake. Jack rewarded. Years later became engine driver and drove the very express that he had saved.

(Matriculation, September 1933)

X

That reminds me of an incident. A few days ago, in a lonely spot near a wood, I met a little boy of about ten years old,[1] who, leaning against a tree trunk, his head hidden in his arms, was crying bitterly. I asked him what was the matter, and after a little difficulty[2] I learned that, having been sent with some money to pay a debt, he had lost it.[3] The poor child did not dare to return home. It was a very serious[4] loss and he knew it. He was afraid to tell his parents what had happened, and he was filled with sorrow at the thought of the harm he had done them. I put my hand in my pocket.

1 *âgé d'une dizaine d'années.* 2 'not without some difficulty.' 3 'that one had sent him...and that he had lost it.' 4 *important* (after noun).

Write about 150 words in French in continuation of the above story but using the third person. You may base your narrative on the following outline:

The man made good the loss—boy's gratitude—man accompanied him to his home, a poor cottage—what he found there—poverty of the family through misfortune—what he did to help them.

(Matriculation, January 1935)

XI

Translate into French:

It was winter and we were all hungry. When supper was ready Mamma called us and we went into the bathroom to wash our hands. Papa had not yet come back and we began the meal without him.

We were always more gay when he was not at home, for although he loved us he could not bear all the noise we made. Mamma served us, and was about to begin her own meal when she suddenly stood up. 'There is your father', she said. 'I can hear his keys.' The door opened and Papa came in, smiling. He had not taken off his hat and overcoat. He was holding a long envelope which he threw on the table.

Write in French about 150 words in continuation of the above story.

Father explains that the letter announces the death of the Mother's aunt, who has left them her money. Mother is sad, but the children are excited and begin to make plans: bigger house, more holidays, etc.

(Matriculation, June 1935)

XII

Translate into French:

My grandfather was travelling in Italy and found himself one evening in the principal inn of a small town. The weather was cold. He was sitting alone at one end of a great dining room and, having finished his meal, was wondering how to spend[1] the rest of the evening. He called the host and asked him for something to read. The host brought him a Bible and a few old English newspapers. While he was reading one of the latter, he heard from time to time bursts of laughter which came from the kitchen. He threw aside the paper and went to look at the people who seemed to be so merry. They were travellers who had arrived some hours before[2] in a coach, and who, seated round the fire, were warming themselves.

1 'how he was going to spend.' 2 *auparavant.*

Write in French about 150 words in continuation of the above story. You may draw on your imagination or use the following outline:

He asks permission to join the travellers—is welcomed by them—discovers an old acquaintance—how the evening was spent—songs and stories—what happened next morning.

(Matriculation, September 1935)

XIII

The Cat's Pilgrimage

Use 2nd Person Singular throughout.

Note. In Exercises XIII, XIV, and XV 'the Cat' should be translated by *la Chatte.*

Translate into French:

'It is all very fine,'[1] said the Cat, 'but I don't see the use of it[2]. . . . I want to learn how to be[3] happy. I would ask the men, only they are so conceited and stupid, they don't understand what we say. I'll ask the Dog.'

'Dog,' said she, 'What do you think of life?'

The Dog opened his eyes, looked sleepily at the Cat, and then shut them again.

'Dog,' said she, 'I want to talk to you. Don't go to sleep. Can't you answer a civil question?'

'Don't bother me', said the Dog. 'I am tired. I stood on my hind legs for ten minutes this morning, before I could get[4] my breakfast, and it hasn't agreed with me[5].'

'Who told you to do it?' said the Cat.

'Why the lady I have to take care of me!' replied the Dog.

'Do you feel any better for it,[6] Dog, after standing on your legs?' said she.

'Haven't I told you, stupid Cat, that it hasn't agreed with me? Let me go to sleep, and don't plague me.'

J. A. FROUDE

1 'all that is very (*fort*) fine.' 2 *à quoi cela peut servir.* 3 § 74 (*b*). 4 *obtenir.* 5 *cela ne m'a pas réussi.* 6 *T'en trouves-tu mieux?*

Continue the story in dialogue form, based on the following résumé:

Cat tells dog that if, instead of sleeping so much, he will listen to the men he will hear them say that cats and dogs are in the world merely to amuse them. Dog answers that he never listens to the men unless they talk about himself. Cat replies that if there is nothing to do but eat and sleep, life is not worth living. She will go and ask the creatures in the woods what one ought to do to be happy. She invites the dog to accompany her, but he prefers to go to sleep on the mat.

XIV

The Cat's Pilgrimage (*continued*)

Use 2nd Person Singular in the conversational parts.

Translate into French:

So[1] the Dog refused to accompany the Cat and she set off by herself[2] to learn how to be happy. It was a fine sunny morning, and she soon heard a blackbird singing under a thornbush. She had had a good breakfast, and she was not hungry, so[3] she could listen to the bird without wanting to eat it.

'Good morning, Blackbird. You seem to be enjoying yourself.'

'Good morning, Cat.'

'Blackbird, it is perhaps an odd question[4]—What must one do to be as happy as you?'

'Do your duty, Cat.'

'But what is my duty?'

'Take care of your little ones[5]!'

'I haven't any.'

'Then sing to your mate.'

'He is dead.'

'Poor cat! Then sing over his grave.'

'No, that isn't cats' nature.[6] When I am cross, I mew, when I am pleased, I purr. But I must be pleased first. I can't make myself happy by purring[7].'

'I am afraid you have a cold heart, Cat. It wants warming[8].'

J. A. Froude

1 *Ainsi.* 2 *seule.* 3 *donc* after *pouvait.* 4 § 3 (*f*). 5 *tes petits.* 6 'in the nature of cats.' 7 *à force de ronronner.* 8 'it has need of being warmed.'

Continue the story in dialogue form, based on the following résumé:

Cat next questions the Ox, who tells her to do her duty by getting her dinner. Cat replies that dinner is prepared for her, she only has to eat it, but is none the happier. Ox tells her she is a wicked ungrateful Cat.

A bee comes buzzing by. Asked what it is doing, it replies it is doing its duty by making honey and expresses surprise that Cat can't make honey and says she must be very stupid. Asks Cat what she does do. Cat replies she can't find anything to do. Bee tells her she is good-for-nothing drone and wishes her good-day.

drone, *le faux-bourdon*.

XV

The Cat's Pilgrimage (*continued*)

Use 2nd Person Singular in the conversation.

Translate into French:

The Cat wandered on,[1] and presently she came to a glade, in the middle of which was seated a fine fat Rabbit.

'Really', said the Cat, 'I don't want to be troublesome. I wouldn't do it, if I could help it,[2] but I am very hungry, I am afraid I must[3] eat you. I assure you it will be just as[4] unpleasant for me as for you.'

The poor Rabbit begged for mercy.

'Well,[5] it is indeed hard. But what can a cat do? You eat the grass, I eat you. But, Rabbit, I wish you would do me a favour.'

'Anything to save my life[6]', said the Rabbit.

'It is not exactly[7] that, but I am not used to killing my own food, and it is disagreeable. Couldn't you die? I shall hurt you dreadfully, if I kill you.'

'Oh', said the Rabbit. 'You are a kind cat. I see it in[8] your eyes. Your whiskers don't curl like those of the wild cats in[9] the woods. I'm sure you will spare my life[10].' J. A. Froude

1 'continued to wander.' 2 help it, *m'en empêcher*. 3 'I am sorry to be obliged to.' 4 *tout aussi*. 5 *Eh, oui*. 6 *Tout pour avoir la vie sauve*. 7 *précisément*. 8 and 9 What preposition in French? 10 *me laisser la vie*.

Continue the conversation, basing it on the following résumé:

Cat says it is a question of duty. Everyone has told her it is her duty to get her dinner. Rabbit answers that if she eats him, he will be unable to do his duty of looking after his seven little ones at home. Cat expresses interest and asks to see them. Rabbit objects, she would eat them. Cat says she couldn't answer for herself, so will let Rabbit go. Asked whether he is happy Rabbit replies that he will indeed be happy, if beautiful Cat spares his little ones.

XVI

J'ai couru tout Paris, disait-il d'une voix sourde, je n'y connais personne, et comment oser demander à des indifférents? Mon vieil ami a été mis en prison, et, d'ailleurs, il m'a prêté tout ce dont il pouvait disposer.

Mais nous n'avons besoin de rien, répondit doucement Ginevra en affectant un air calme.

Chaque jour qui arrive amène une difficulté de plus, reprit Luigi avec terreur.

Luigi prit tous les tableaux de Ginevra, le portrait, plusieurs meubles desquels le ménage pouvait encore se passer, il vendit tout à vil prix, et la somme qu'il en obtint prolongea l'agonie du ménage pendant quelques moments. Dans ces jours de malheur, Ginevra, supportant tous les maux, était même heureuse encore quand elle voyait sur les lèvres de Luigi un sourire d'étonnement à l'aspect de la propreté qu'elle faisait régner dans l'unique chambre où ils s'étaient réfugiés.

Write in French about 150 words in continuation of the above story. You may draw on your imagination or use the following outline:

A few days later Luigi perceives that Ginevra and their son are dying of hunger. He determines to sell matches in the streets. Returning home with empty pocket he saves from being killed by a runaway horse the wife of a wealthy American business man, who finds Luigi work in the United States. Happiness in new home.

(Matriculation, January 1932)

XVII

Arrivé à Versailles, je me dirigeai vers le château. Au vestiaire, qui est près de la chapelle, je confiai au gardien mon parapluie, et je montai le petit escalier qui mène aux grands appartements. Je me trouvai bientôt dans la pièce qui fut la chambre à coucher du roi. Vous connaissez, au chevet du lit, l'étonnant portrait en cire qui représente Louis XIV âgé. Je m'approchai pour regarder le visage royal qui montre, sous l'abondante perruque, son profil orgueilleux. Je serais resté là longtemps, à contempler l'image royale, si un groupe de touristes, accompagnés par un guide à casquette, ne fût venu troubler ma rêverie....

Lorsque j'eus repris mon parapluie et que je me trouvai sur la terrasse du château, j'eus un moment d'hésitation. Le ciel s'était couvert. Les rares promeneurs se hâtaient. Je crus même sentir quelques gouttes de pluie. Néanmoins, malgré le temps menaçant, il m'en coûtait de ne pas pousser jusqu'aux jardins de Trianon.

HENRI DE RÉGNIER

Translate into French:

I had often visited these gardens in autumn and even in winter, but I had never found them so deserted. I did not meet anybody during the first quarter-of-an-hour of my walk. As it was fine now, I sat down on a stone bench to rest a little.

Five minutes later I thought I heard footsteps, and raising my eyes I saw an old man who was walking slowly towards me.[1] He was wearing a black coat and a wide hat which hid his face from me; and though he passed quite close to me he did not seem to see me.

Soon afterwards a distant[2] clock struck four; and as it had begun to rain I decided to return at once to the station.

1 'approaching me with (*à*) slow steps.' 2 *lointain*.

Continue the story in French, using the following outline:

A cab passes and the narrator gets in. The same old man appears and accepts a lift. On catching sight of his profile his companion is astonished to see that it exactly resembles that of Louis XIV. The old man gets out at the palace and courteously offers a coin as his share of the fare. The narrator is afterwards amazed to find it is dated 1701 and bears the effigy of Louis XIV.

(General School, Midsummer 1933)

XVIII

C'est singulier, je ne m'y reconnais plus. J'ai pourtant fait l'ascension du Parmelan autrefois.

Oui, il y a vingt-cinq ou trente ans, oncle César, interrompit d'une voix légèrement moqueuse l'une des jeunes filles.

Mais depuis trente ans les bois ont grandi et votre mémoire n'en a pas fait autant. Le sentier s'est peut-être déplacé?

Tais-toi, Françoise! repartit l'oncle d'un ton de mauvaise humeur. Ma mémoire est excellente, seulement dans cette obscurité je ne me retrouve plus.

Vous auriez dû m'écouter et prendre un guide à Dingy, répliqua Françoise en secouant les épaules avec un geste d'enfant gâtée. Ça ne serait pas gai de coucher à la belle étoile!

Moi, j'en prendrais bien mon parti, dit à son tour la seconde jeune fille; regarde, c'est vraiment beau.

Write in French a continuation of the above story. You may use your imagination or draw on the following outline:

A shepherd indicated the right path—journey continued up the mountain in the darkness—meeting with young traveller with lantern—arrival at summit—supper at the chalet—short sleep—beauty of sunrise in snow-covered Alps.

(Matriculation, June 1933)

XIX

L'homme reparut avec sa lanterne, tirant au bout d'une corde un cheval triste qui ne venait pas volontiers. Il le plaça contre le timon[1], et marcha longtemps autour pour assurer les harnais, en portant sa lumière à la main. Comme il allait chercher la seconde bête, il remarqua tous ses voyageurs immobiles, déjà blancs de neige, et leur dit: 'Pourquoi ne montez-vous pas dans la voiture? Vous serez à l'abri au moins.' Ils n'y avaient pas songé, sans doute, et ils s'y précipitèrent. Les trois hommes installèrent leurs femmes dedans et montèrent ensuite; puis les autres gens prirent à leur tour les dernières places sans échanger une parole. Enfin, la diligence étant attelée avec six chevaux, une voix du dehors demanda: 'Tout le monde est-il monté?' On répondit: 'Oui', et on partit.

1 *le timon*, the shaft.

After reading through the above passage write in French about 150 words in continuation of the story, using the following outline:

Journey along bad roads in thick snow and darkness—discomfort of passengers—accident—wheel came off—two horses fell—hunger and bad temper of travellers and driver—difficulties of walk to inn several miles away—food and warmth restored good humour.

(Matriculation, September 1934)

XX

À la porte Georges recontra Monsieur André et il l'accompagna quelques pas. Quand l'avocat et l'enfant se séparèrent, celui-ci s'avisa qu'il arriverait en retard chez son oncle. Il voulut regarder l'heure. Alors seulement il s'aperçut que sa poche était vide. Cette découverte l'effraya. Fiévreusement, et en examinant toutes les pierres du trottoir, il reprit le chemin qu'il venait de faire. Arrivé devant la maison de Jacques, il se rappela qu'il avait tiré sa montre pour la donner à regarder à son ami. Il gravit l'escalier quatre à quatre, avec l'espoir, avec la certitude presque de retrouver aussitôt le précieux objet. Lorsqu'il entra dans la chambre, Jacques fit semblant de se réveiller. Il se leva, secoua les couvertures, l'oreiller, et dit après ces recherches: 'Il me semble bien que tu as remis la montre dans la poche de ton gilet.'

Write in French about 150 words in continuation of the above story. You may draw on your imagination or use the following outline:

George's confession of the loss to his uncle who had given him the watch—his uncle's questions—further search—where and how it was found.

(Matriculation, June 1936)

(4) LETTER WRITING

ON THE ENVELOPE

(1) Write Monsieur, Madame, Mademoiselle in full. The abbreviations M., Mme, Mlle are only used in commercial style.

(2) rue is generally written with a small letter, Avenue and Boulevard in capitals.

(3) The number 7 should have a stroke through it, 7, to distinguish it from 1 which often resembles a 7.

(4) On a letter for Paris the number of the arrondissement should be given in Roman numerals, e.g. xvme.

(5) In provincial addresses the name of the department is usually given in round brackets, e.g. St Étienne (Loire).

(6) Local = En Ville.

(7) Please forward = Prière de faire suivre, or simply Faire suivre.

(8) For the sake of security the name and address of the sender are often written on the back of the envelope, prefixed by the word Expéditeur (sender).

IN THE LETTER

In dates the names of the months begin with a small letter, e.g. le 31 janvier.

Modes of Address

Dear Sir	Monsieur
	Monsieur le Directeur (to the Manager of a hotel, etc.)
	Monsieur le Chef de Gare (to a station master)
Dear Madam	Madame
	Mademoiselle
Dear Mr Smith (less formal)	Cher Monsieur
,, Mrs ,, ,,	Chère Madame

Between members of the same profession:

(My) Dear Colleague	(Mon) Cher Collègue

Between relations:

(My) Dear Father	(Mon) Cher papa
(My) Dear Mother	(Ma) Chère maman
Dear Aunt Lucy	Chère tante Lucie
(My) Dear Henry	(Mon) Cher Henri

Beginning of a Letter

Je reçois à l'instant votre lettre du 1er courant
I have just received your letter of the 1st inst.
Merci bien de votre bonne lettre
Many thanks for your kind letter

Je suis très heureux d'avoir de vos nouvelles
I am very glad to have news of you
Je regrette d'avoir tant tardé à répondre
I am sorry to have been so long in replying

Je viens vous demander...
I am writing to ask you...

Closing words of a letter

À bientôt de vos nouvelles Dans l'espoir de vous lire (Commercial)	Hoping to hear from you soon
Faites mes amitiés à votre frère Rappelez-moi au bon souvenir de votre frère	Remember me kindly to your brother

Mes parents se joignent à moi pour vous envoyer leurs meilleurs souvenirs
My parents join me in sending their kindest remembrances

Meilleures amitiés à tout le monde	Love to all
Amitiés à tout le monde	Kind regards to all

Signature

There are many different ways of concluding a letter in French in order to express varying degrees of familiarity and affection. The following are some of the expressions in most common use:

Yours faithfully (business letters)	Agréez, Monsieur, mes salutations empressées

Yours truly (formal)	Veuillez agréer, Monsieur, l'expression de mes sentiments les meilleurs
Yours very truly (slightly less formal)	Croyez, Monsieur, à ma considération distinguée
Yours sincerely (between people of the same social status who already know each other)	Croyez-moi bien, cher Monsieur, votre dévoué or simply, Votre dévoué

To a lady:

(formal) Veuillez agréer, Madame, l'assurance de mes sentiments respectueux

(less formal) Veuillez agréer, Madame, l'expression de mes sentiments dévoués

Between friends:	Bien à vous (toi) Bien cordialement à vous (toi)
Between girl friends:	Bien affectueusement à toi
Your affectionate son	Ton fils affectionné
Yours affectionately	Ton affectionné(e)

N.B. The Past Indefinite (Perfect) must be used to describe past events. The Past Definite is not used in Letter Writing.

LETTRES

(1)

Écrivez à un jeune Français (une jeune Française) pour lui proposer un échange de correspondance.

perfectionner son français, improve one's French
faire des progrès, get on, make progress
corriger des fautes, correct mistakes
échanger des impressions, exchange impressions
le corrigé, fair copy
faire la description du pays, describe the country
la vie scolaire, life at school
les occupations, pursuits, hobbies
les heures de classe, school hours
les vacances, holidays

(2)

Écrivez à un(e) ami(e) pour l'inviter à venir passer les grandes vacances (summer holidays) au bord de la mer. Dites-lui quelles distractions vous pouvez lui offrir.

(3)

Vous allez vous présenter à (go in for) un examen.

Écrivez une lettre à vos parents pour leur dire quelles sont vos chances de succès.

Indiquez les principaux sujets que vous étudiez.

être fort en, be strong in
points faibles, weak points
les examinateurs, examiners
les candidats, candidates
les épreuves, (set) papers
être reçu, pass
échouer, fail
une bonne note, good marks
une mauvaise note, bad marks
passable, fair, pretty good

(4)

Vous avez deux billets de théâtre (ou de cinéma) dont vous ne pouvez pas vous servir.

Écrivez une lettre à un(e) ami(e) pour lui offrir ces deux billets, en lui indiquant le genre de pièce (ou de film) qu'on va représenter.

de bonnes places, good seats
au premier rang, in the first row
premier balcon, dress circle
fauteuils d'orchestre, stalls
une pièce très courue, very popular play
acteur (actrice) préféré(e), favourite actor (actress),
au premier acte, in the first act
voici l'intrigue, here is the plot
il s'agit de, it is about
jouer le rôle, play the part
avoir le rôle d'étoile, play a 'star' role
les personnages, characters
l'action se passe, the scene is laid
applaudir vivement, applaud loudly

(5)

Écrivez à la direction d'un hôtel situé au bord de la mer pour demander qu'on vous réserve deux chambres à un lit à partir du 1er août. Dites combien de temps vous comptez y rester. Demandez des renseignements (1) sur la ville et les distractions qu'elle offre aux visiteurs, (2) sur l'hôtel, son jardin, sa situation, sa distance de la plage.

Voir p. 131 et servez-vous des expressions suivantes:

disponible, free (of rooms)
retenir, engage
le prix de pension, boarding terms
un séjour d'une quinzaine de jours, a fortnight's stay
avec eau courante, with running water
au premier étage, on the first storey
avec vue sur la mer, with sea view
à peu de distance de, at a short distance from

(6)

Écrivez à un chef de gare pour lui annoncer la perte d'une petite valise que vous avez laissée dans un compartiment de chemin de fer. Faites la description de la valise et demandez si on l'a trouvée.

en cuir, leather
serrure nickelée, nickel-plated lock
initiales (f.), initials
articles de toilette, toilet articles
indicateur de chemin de fer, railway time-table
par mégarde, inadvertently
guide des environs, guide to the neighbourhood
en souffrance, waiting to be called for

(7)

Écrivez une lettre en réponse à une agence de tourisme qui demande un(e) employé(e) ayant une bonne connaissance de la dactylographie et deux langues modernes.

être bon(ne) dactylographe, be a good typist
écrire une lettre à la machine, typewrite a letter
sténographier, take down in shorthand
savoir une langue à fond, know a language thoroughly
savoir passablement le français, know French fairly well
parler couramment le français, speak French fluently
vous donner satisfaction, give you satisfaction

(8)

Le jour de la distribution des prix (Prize-giving Day).

Écrivez une lettre à vos parents pour leur faire la description de la cérémonie et des fêtes qui l'ont suivie.

le Directeur, Headmaster
l'estrade (f.), platform
l'assistance (f.), audience
faire un discours, make a speech
distribuer les prix, distribute the prizes
décerner le prix, award the prize
remporter le prix, win the prize
applaudir vivement, applaud loudly
représenter, perform
le bal, ball
en grande toilette (of ladies), in their best dresses
avoir lieu, take place
la Directrice, Headmistress
la salle, hall
un livre de prix, prize book
la pièce, play
le garden-party, garden party
se dérouler, be enacted (of ceremonies, etc.)

(9)

Vous allez passer un mois en France chez les Dupont.

Écrivez une lettre à Madame Dupont lui annonçant la date probable de votre arrivée et l'itinéraire que vous comptez suivre. Dites-lui que vous espérez perfectionner votre connaissance du français et expliquez-lui quels progrès vous avez déjà faits dans cette langue. Demandez des renseignements sur le pays environnant et informez-vous s'il y aura des occasions de jouer au tennis et de faire de la bicyclette.

je compte arriver, I expect to arrive
préciser la date, give the exact date
vous fixer à ce sujet, let you know definitely about this
veuillez me faire savoir, kindly let me know
les routes accidentées, hilly roads
les routes plates, flat roads
apporter sa raquette, bring one's racket

(10)

Réponse de Madame Dupont à la lettre ci-dessus.

(5) CONVERSATION

(1) The Perfect must be used in place of the Past Definite, e.g. I saw—j'ai vu. I went—je suis allé.

(2) Questions can often be expressed by an affirmative clause with a mark of interrogation, e.g. Vous croyez? Do you think so?

Likes and Dislikes.

Cela vous plaît?	Do you like that?
Cela vous intéresse?	Are you interested in it?
Cela } ne me sourit guère	I don't like that very much
Cette idée } ne me sourit guère	,, ,, that idea much
Cela ne me dit rien	That (it) doesn't appeal to me
,, ,, pas grande chose	,, ,, much appeal to me
J'adore la musique	I am very fond of music
Je suis passionné pour le théâtre	I am very keen on the theatre
Il est passionné pour le cinéma	He is a cinema fan
Je déteste le froid }	I hate the cold
J'ai horreur du froid }	
Ce n'est pas à mon goût	It is not to my taste
Chacun à son goût	Everyone to his own taste

Opinions.

Avoir raison Be right	Avoir tort Be wrong
Il me semble que	It seems to me that
À mon avis } In my opinion	
À mon idée }	
Je suis de votre avis	I am of your opinion
Je suis d'accord	I agree with you
D'accord!	Granted! Quite so!
Je soutiens que	I maintain that
Je ne crois pas que + subj.	I don't think that...
Mettons que vous ayez raison	Supposing you are right
Je crois que oui I think so	Je crois que non I think not
Je ne crois pas	I don't think so

J'ai bien peur que non	I am afraid not
Qu'en dites-vous?	What do you say about it?
Comment le trouvez-vous?	What do you think of it?

Affirmation and Denial.

Parfaitement	Exactly (so)	Absolument	Quite so
Naturellement	Of course	Bien sûr!	I should think so!
Nullement	By no means	Non certes	Certainly not
C'est ça (approval)	That's it / That's right	Au contraire	On the contrary

Questions and Exclamations.

Comment? What? Plaît-il? I beg your pardon?
À la bonne heure! Good! Capital! Splendid!
Voyons! Come now! Allons donc! Nonsense!
Tiens! tiens! Indeed! You don't say so!
Par exemple (surprise) Fancy that! Well, I never!
Par exemple (intensive) C'est loin, par exemple! It's a long way, and no mistake

CONVERSATION EXERCISES

(1)

Conversation entre un voyageur et un douanier (custom house officer).

Avez-vous quelque chose à déclarer? Have you anything to declare?
Articles défendus: tabac—cigares—cigarettes—allumettes—dentelle (lace)—vins—spiritueux (spirits).

payer le droits, pay duties
payer une amende, pay a fine
une petite provision de, a small amount of
fouiller dans, rummage about in
autre chose, anything else
une valise, suit-case
une malle, trunk
au fond de, at the bottom of
fermé à clef, locked
rien d'autre, nothing else

(2)

Conversation entre un Anglais et un Français dans un compartiment de chemin de fer. Le Français veut qu'on ferme la glace (window), l'Anglais tient à ce qu'elle reste ouverte.

l'air frais, fresh air
respirer, breathe
on étouffe, it is stifling
asphyxié, suffocated
malsain, unhealthy
vous autres Anglais, you English
le courant d'air, draught
la porte du couloir, door of the corridor
mourir de froid, die of cold
gelé, frozen
insupportable, unbearable

(3)

Dialogue entre deux amis, dont l'un préfère les pays chauds et l'autre les pays froids.

la luminosité du ciel, the clear atmosphere
les paysages ensoleillés, sunny landscapes
les longues siestes d'après-midi, long afternoon siestas
les repas servis en plein air, meals served in the open air
dormir à la belle étoile, sleep in the open air
les vêtements légers, light clothes
être frileux, feel the cold
les sports d'hiver, winter sports
les fortes gelées, hard frosts
les longues nuits d'hiver, long winter nights
au coin du feu, by the fireside
la lecture et la T.S.F., reading and wireless
le patinage, skating
faire des glissades, make slides
faire du toboggan, go tobogganing

(4)

La scène se passe dans un grand magasin (stores). Racontez la conversation qui s'engage entre un employé et vous-même au sujet d'un cadeau que vous allez choisir pour un ami (une amie) à l'occasion de son anniversaire.

On s'occupe de vous, Monsieur? Are they attending to you, sir?
Madame désire? What can I do for you, Madam?
il me faut..., I want...
Combien cet article? How much is this article?
en magasin, in stock
Combien c'est? How much is it?
Quel genre de...? What kind of?

dans ce genre-là, of that kind

Vous en avez d'autres? Have you any others?

quelque chose de moins cher, something cheaper

à un prix plus avantageux, at a lower price

Et avec ça, Madame? And the next, please

payer à la caisse, pay at the desk

(5)

Un jeune Français (une jeune Française) vient passer les vacances chez vous. Racontez votre première conversation avec le nouvel arrivé (la nouvelle arrivée).

(6)

Dialogue entre un cocher de fiacre et un chauffeur de taxi.

(7)

Conversation entre deux jeunes filles, dont l'une veut entrer dans les affaires et l'autre aime mieux rester chez elle à faire le ménage.

(8)

Conversation entre deux fervents du cinéma, dont l'un préfère les films anglais et l'autre les films américains.

(9)

Dialogue entre un agent de police et un(e) automobiliste qui vient de dépasser le signal lumineux au moment où la lumière rouge s'est montrée.

(10)

C'est votre premier voyage en France. Vous êtes dans un compartiment de chemin de fer entre Calais (ou Boulogne ou Dieppe) et Paris. Dans le compartiment se trouvent un Français et sa femme.

Racontez la conversation, qui s'engage entre vous-même et vos compagnons de voyage.

(6) MISCELLANEOUS

Lors d'une visite en France votre ami français, Lucien (votre amie française, Lucette), vous a prié (priée) de lui trouver, en Angleterre, un emploi, afin de se perfectionner en langue anglaise. Écrivez-lui en français une lettre (120 mots, maximum) lui indiquant l'emploi que vous avez trouvé, le genre de travail et les conditions.

(Northern Universities Joint Matriculation, July 1929)

You are in France on a visit. One day Madame Roger, your hostess, is too unwell to do her shopping. The servant is busy. Shopping must be done. You have to do it. Your hostess explains:

'Si vous voulez bien faire mes petites commissions, dont voici la liste, vous serez bien aimable. Venez donc la voir; il faut aller chez le boucher, l'épicier, et le pharmacien, et aussi au bureau de poste, mais vous n'avez pas besoin de payer comptant chez les deux premiers. Voici un billet de cent francs.'

Write in French (120 words, maximum) what you say to Mme Roger on your return, giving an account of your shopping expedition.

(Northern Universities Joint Matriculation, July 1930)

Vous allez à Paris passer les vacances de Noël chez des amis. De Calais à Paris il y a dans votre compartiment de chemin de fer trois personnes—une vieille dame, un jeune Français et vous-même.

Write in French (120 words, maximum) a description of your fellow-passengers and the incidents of the journey.

N.B. Do not use the present tense unless the persons in the carriage are conversing one with another.

(Northern Universities Joint Matriculation, July 1931)

On vous a fait cadeau de vingt francs (5*s*.).

Write in French, using not less than 110 words and not more than 130, a description of your visit to the shops and the way in which you spent this money.

Do not use the present tense except for conversations.

(Northern Universities Matriculation, July 1938)

Vous envoyez un chien dont vous voulez vous débarrasser à un parent qui habite à une distance de trois heures en chemin de fer. Deux jours après, le chien est de retour chez vous, ayant retrouvé tout seul son chemin.

Describe in French, using not less than 110 words, and not more than 130, the dog's return and say whether you decide to keep him.

N.B. Do not use the present tense except for conversation. Count your words and state the number.

(Northern Universities Matriculation, September 1933)

Write in French not less than 110 words and not more than 130 words on the following subject:

Racontez une visite que vous avez faite au bord de la mer ou à la campagne—votre départ—ce que vous avez vu—comment vous avez sauvé la vie à votre ami(e)—votre retour.

N.B. Your narration must be mainly in the *perfect* (past indefinite), as in the above outline.

(Northern Universities Matriculation, September 1934)

Write in French not less than 110 words and not more than 130 words on the following subject:

Votre père vous a donné une bicyclette pour votre fête. Racontez une journée pendant les vacances que vous avez passées avec votre ami(e).

(Northern Universities Matriculation, July 1935)

Section IV

GENERAL VOCABULARY

omitting numerals, days of the week and months of the year

Composite expressions will generally be found under the first word of the expression, e.g. 'get hungry' under 'get', 'summer holidays' under 'summer', etc.

ABBREVIATIONS

adj.	=adjective	inf.	=infinitive	past def.	=past definite
adv.	=adverb	interrog.	=interrogative	plur.	=plural
conj.	=conjunction	intrans.	=intransitive	prep.	=preposition
exclam.	=exclamation	invar.	=invariable	pron.	=pronoun
f.	=feminine	m.	=masculine	relat.	=relative
indef.	=indefinite	n.	=noun	subj.	=subjunctive
indic.	=indicative	obj.	=object	trans.	=transitive

p.=page §§ refer to sections in Syntax

abandon, *renoncer à*
able, be —, *pouvoir*
about (concerning), *à propos de, au sujet de*
about (around), *autour de*
about (of time), *vers*
about, be — to, *être sur le point de*
above, prep. *au-dessus de*
above all, *avant tout, surtout*
absence, *l'absence* f.
absent, *absent*
absent-minded, *distrait*
absolutely, *absolument*
absolutely none, *absolument aucun(e)*
absorb, *absorber*
absorbed in (doing), *occupé à (faire)*, in Ex. xxxiv, p. 100, use *absorber*
absurd, *absurde*
accelerator, *l'accélérateur* m.
accept, *accepter*
accident, *l'accident* m.
accompany, *accompagner*
accomplished, *cultivé*

accordingly, *conséquemment*
account, on — of, *à cause de, par suite de*
acquaintance, *la connaissance*
act, in the — of, *en train de* + inf.
add, *ajouter*
address, n. *l'adresse* f.
address, vb. (a letter), *adresser,* (a person) *s'adresser à, adresser la parole à*
admirably, *admirablement*
admire, *admirer*
admit, *admettre*
advance, *s'avancer*
advantage, *l'avantage* m.
adventure, *l'aventure* f.
advertise, *annoncer*
advice, *le conseil*
advise, *conseiller (à quelqu'un de faire quelque chose)*
aeroplane, *l'avion* m.; **in an —,** *en avion*
affectionate, *affectionné*
afraid, be —, *avoir peur* ('to do' or 'of doing', *de* + inf.); **be — that,** *avoir peur que...ne* + subj.
after, prep. and adv. *après*
after all, *après tout*
after that, *ensuite*
afternoon, *l'après-midi* m. or f.
again, *de nouveau*
against, *contre*
age, *l'âge* m.
Agnes, *Agnès*
ago, an hour —, *il y a une heure*
agreeable, *agréable*
ail, what ails you? *qu'avez-vous donc?*
air, *l'air* m.
airman, *l'aviateur* m.
Alexandria, *Alexandrie*
alight, *descendre*
alive, *vivant*
all, *tout, toute, tous, toutes*
all along, *tout le long de*
all at once, *tout à coup*
all over (p. 120), *partout en*
all right, *ça va bien*
all round, adv. *tout autour*; prep. *tout autour de*
allow, *permettre (à quelqu'un de faire quelque chose)*
almost, *presque*
alone, *seul*
along, *le long de*
aloud, *à haute voix*
Alps, *les Alpes* f.
already, *déjà*
alter, *changer*
although, *bien que* + subj.
always, *toujours*
amazement, in —, *tout ébahi*
America, *l'Amérique* f.
American, *américain*; **an —,** *un Américain*
among, *parmi*; **— other things,** *entre autres choses*
amuse oneself by (doing), *s'amuser à (faire)*
amusing, *amusant*
angrily, *en colère*
angry, *fâché*; **be —,** *être en colère, être fâché*; **become —,** *se mettre en colère*

animal, *l'animal* m.
announce, *annoncer*
announcer (wireless), *le speaker*
annoy, *vexer*
another, *un(e) autre*
answer, n. *la réponse*
answer, vb. *répondre,* (a person) *répondre à (quelqu'un)*
anxious, be — to, *tenir à* + inf.; **be particularly — to,** *tenir beaucoup à*
anxiously, *d'un ton inquiet*
any, adj. (in questions and after *si*) *quelque,* (in negative phrases) *ne...aucun(e)*
any, not —, (of quantity) *ne... pas de*
any, pron. *en*
any amount of, *énormément de*
any more, plur. adj. *d'autres*
any of the..., (in negative expressions) *aucun(e) des...*
anybody, not —, *ne...personne*
anyone who, *quiconque*
anything, (in questions and after *si*) *quelque chose*; **not... anything,** *ne...rien*
apartment, *l'appartement* m.
apologize profusely, *se confondre en excuses*
appear, *paraître*
appease, *apaiser*
appetite, have a good —, *avoir bon appétit*
apply, *appliquer*; **— the brakes,** *serrer les freins*
appointment, make an —, *donner (un) rendez-vous*; **miss an —,** *manquer un rendez-vous*
approach, *s'approcher de, approcher de*
archly, *d'un ton espiègle*
arise, *se lever*
aristocracy, *l'aristocratie* f.
Arkville, *Archeville*
arm, n. *le bras*
arm, vb. *armer*
armchair, *le fauteuil*
arrange, *arranger*
arrange for, *prendre des dispositions pour que* + subj.
arrival, *l'arrivée* f.; **on his** or **her —,** *à son arrivée*
arrive, *arriver*
article, *l'objet* m.
artist, *l'artiste* m.
as, *comme*
as far as, prep. *jusqu'à*
as if + finite verb, *comme si* + indic.
as much as, *autant que*
as soon as, *aussitôt que, dès que*
as soon as possible, *le plus tôt possible*
as though (with finite verb), *comme si* + indic.
as usual, *comme d'habitude*
ascertain, *s'assurer*
ask, *demander*; **— someone,** *demander à quelqu'un*; **— someone for a thing,** *demander une chose à quelqu'un*; **— someone to** (do), *demander à quelqu'un de (faire)*

ask a question, *poser une question (à quelqu'un)*
ask for, *demander* + direct obj.
ask to, *demander à* + inf.
asleep, *endormi*
assert, *prétendre*
assistant, *le commis*
assure, *assurer*
astonished, *étonné*; **much —,** *très étonné*
astonishment, *l'étonnement* m.
at any moment, *d'un moment à l'autre*
at first, *d'abord*
at home, *chez moi, chez lui*, etc.
at last, *enfin*
at least, *au moins*
at length, *enfin*
at once, *tout de suite*
at present, *à présent*
at the same time (as), *en même temps (que)*
attack, n. *l'attaque* f.
attack, vb. *attaquer*
attend, *assister à*
attend to, *s'occuper de*
attention! *attention!*
attention, *l'attention* f.; **pay — to,** *faire attention à*
attract, *attirer*
aunt, *la tante*
Australia, *l'Australie*
autograph album, *l'album d'autographes*
automatic system, *le système automatique*
autumn, in—, *en automne*
avoid (doing), *éviter (de faire)*
await, *attendre*
awake, trans. *réveiller*, intrans. *se réveiller*
awake, remain —, *rester éveillé*
away, *absent*
awful, *affreux*
awfully, *rudement*
awfully sorry, *désolé* ('to' = *de* + inf.)

back, n. *le dos*
back, be —, *être de retour*; **so you're —,** *te voilà de retour*
backwards and forwards, *de long en large*
bacon, *le lard*
badge, *la plaque*
bag, *le sac*
baggage, *les bagages* m.
ball (dance), *le bal*
ball (golf, hockey), *la balle*
ball (football), *le ballon*
ballroom, *la salle de bal*
band, *la musique*
bank, *le talus*; **on the — of,** *au bord de*
barber, *le coiffeur*
bare, *nu* (after noun)
bargain, *l'affaire* f.
bark, *aboyer*
barrel organ, *l'orgue de Barbarie (orgue* m.)
basement, *le sous-sol*
basket, *la corbeille*
bath, n. *le bain*
bathe, n. **have a —,** *prendre un bain*
bathroom, *la salle des bains*

beam, *la poutre*
bear, *supporter*
beard, *la barbe*
beat, *battre*
beautiful, *beau* (before vowel or 'h' mute, *bel*), *belle*
beauty, *la beauté*
because, *parce que*
become, *devenir*
become angry, *se mettre en colère*
become enrolled, *se faire inscrire*
become tired, *se fatiguer*
bed, *le lit*; **in —,** *au lit*; **go to —,** *aller se coucher, aller au lit*
bedroom, *la chambre*
beer, *la bière*
before, (of time) *avant,* (with inf.) *avant de*, conj. *avant que*
before (of place), *devant*
beforehand, *à l'avance*
beg, *prier*; **— someone to,** *prier quelqu'un de* + inf.
beg for mercy, *demander grâce*
beggar, *le mendiant*
begin, *commencer* ('to' = *à* + inf.)
begin again, *recommencer*
begin again to, *se remettre à* + inf.
behaviour, *la conduite*
behind, prep. and adv. *derrière*
believe, *croire*
believe in, *croire à*
bell, *la cloche*; **the — rings,** *on sonne*
belong to, *appartenir à*
bench, *le banc*
beneath, *au-dessous de*
bent, *courbé*
berth, *le lit*
beside, prep. *à côté de*
best, adj. *le meilleur*; adv. *le mieux*
better, adj. *meilleur*; adv. *mieux*; **something —,** *quelque chose de mieux*; **be —** (in health), *aller mieux*; **it is — to,** *il vaut mieux* + inf.; **we had —,** *nous ferions mieux de* + inf., see § 68
between, *entre*
bible, *la bible*
bicycle, *la bicyclette, le vélo*; **on bicycles,** *à bicyclette*
big, *gros,* (of a hotel or meal) *grand*
bird, *l'oiseau* m.
biscuit, *le biscuit*
bit, a —, *un peu*
bitterly, *amèrement*; **weep —,** *pleurer à chaudes larmes*
blackbird, *le merle*
blade of grass, *le brin d'herbe*
blanket, *la couverture*
blast on the horn, *le coup de trompe*
blaze, *flamber*
blind, adj. *aveugle*
blind, n. *le store*
blood, *le sang*
blown, be —, (of a horn) *sonner*
blue, *bleu*; **in —,** *en bleu*
Blunderbuss, *Tromblon*
boat, *le bateau*
bogey (golf), *le bogey*

boil, *bouillir*; **— with rage,** *bouillir de colère*
bolt, vb. *fermer au verrou, verrouiller*
book, *le livre*
book, vb. (e.g. a room), *retenir*
bookshop, *la librairie*
bother, *ennuyer*
bottle, *la bouteille*
boy, *le garçon,* (at school) *l'élève*
bow, *le salut*
bowl along, *rouler sur*
box, *la boîte*
brakes, apply the —, *serrer les freins*
brandy, *le cognac*
brave, *brave, courageux*
bread, *le pain*; **— and butter,** *le pain beurré*
break, *casser*; **— the spell,** *rompre le charme*
breakfast, *le petit déjeuner, le déjeuner*
bridge, *le pont*
brigadier, *le brigadier*
bright, it is —, *il fait clair*
brightly, *clair*
bring, (a person) *conduire, amener,* (a thing) *apporter*
bring about, *amener*
bring back (a thing), *rapporter*
bring up, *élever*
Brittany, *la Bretagne*
broad, *large*
broadcast, n. *l'émission* f.
broadcast, vb. *radiodiffuser*
brother, *le frère*
brown, *brun,* (of a cow) *roux, rousse*
build, *construire, bâtir*
building, *le bâtiment*
bull-fight, *la course de taureaux*
bun, *la brioche*
burglar, *le cambrioleur*
burst into sobs, *éclater en sanglots*
burst into tears, *fondre en larmes*
burst of laughter, *l'éclat de rire* m.
burst open, *enfoncer*
business, *les affaires* f.; **a long —,** *une longue affaire*
busy, *occupé*; **a — day,** *une journée très remplie*
busy oneself with, *s'occuper de*
butcher, *le boucher*
butter, *le beurre*; **bread and —,** *le pain beurré*
button, *le bouton*
button up, *boutonner*
buy, *acheter*
by, prep. *par*
by (near), *près de*; **— the fire,** *auprès du feu*
by now, *déjà*
by-the-by, *à propos*

cabin (of aeroplane), *la carlingue*
café, *le café*
cage, *la cage*
Cairo, *le Caire*; **of —,** *du Caire*
calendar, *le calendrier*

call, n. *l'appel* m.; **a — on the horn**, *un appel de trompe*
call, vb. *appeler*; **be called** (by name), *s'appeler*
call at, *passer chez*
call back, *rappeler*
call out, *crier*
call-box, *la cabine téléphonique*
calm, n. *le calme*
calm, vb., **— oneself**, *se calmer*
calmly, *avec calme*
can, vb. *pouvoir*
candle, *la bougie*
captain, *le capitaine*
car, *l'auto* f., *la voiture*
card, *la carte*
care, n. *le soin*; **take — of**, *prendre soin de*; **take — to**, *avoir* or *prendre soin de* + inf.
care for, *soigner*
careful, *prudent*
carriage, *la voiture*
carry, *porter*
carry away, *emporter*
cart, *la charrette*
carter, *le charretier*
case, in that —, *en ce cas-là*; **in such a —**, *en pareil cas*
cast, *jeter*
castle, *le château*
catch (a train), *prendre*
catch fire, *prendre feu*
catch sight of, *apercevoir*
cellar, *la cave*
century, *le siècle*
ceremonious, *cérémonieux*
ceremony, *la cérémonie*
certain, *certain*
certainly, *certainement*
chair, *la chaise*
chaise, *la chaise*
chance, there's no — that, *il n'y a pas de chance pour que* + subj.
change of air, *le changement d'air*
Channel, *la Manche*
chapter, *le chapitre*
charged with, *chargé de*
charm, n. *le charme*
charm, vb. *charmer*
charming, *charmant*
chase, *la chasse*
chat, *causer*
chatter, *bavarder*
chattering, adj. *bavard*
cheek, *la joue*
cheer, *applaudir*
cheer up, *réconforter*
cherry, *la cerise*
chicken, *le poulet*
chiefly, *avant tout*
child, *un* or *une enfant*
childhood, *l'enfance* f.
China tea, *le thé de Chine*
chocolate, *le chocolat*
choose, *choisir*
Christmas, *Noël*; **at —**, *à Noël*; **— Day**, *le jour de Noël*; **— morning**, *le matin de Noël*; **— present**, *le cadeau de Noël*; **last —**, *l'an dernier à Noël*
church, *l'église* f.
cigar, *le cigare*
cigarette, *la cigarette*
cigarette box, *la boîte à cigarettes*

Cinderella, *Cendrillon*
Cingalese, *cingalais*
circle, n., **in a —,** *en cercle*
circle, vb. *tourner en cercle*
circumstance, *la circonstance*
citizeness, *la citoyenne*
city, *la cité*
city man, *l'homme de la cité*
civil, *civile*
clap one's hands, *battre des mains*
class, *la classe*
clean, adj. *propre*
clean, vb. *nettoyer*
clear, *clair*
clearing, *la clairière*
clerk, *l'employé* m.; **lady —,** *l'employée*
climate, *le climat*
climb, n. *la montée*
climb into, *monter dans*
cloak, *le manteau*
clock, (of public buildings) *l'horloge* f., (in a room) *la pendule*
close, vb. *fermer*
close to, prep. *près de*; **quite— —,** *tout près de*
closely, followed —, *suivi de près*
closing, *la fermeture*; **— hours,** *les heures de fermeture*; **— time,** *l'heure de fermeture*
cloth, a piece of —, *un morceau d'étoffe*
clothe, *revêtir* ('in' = *de*)
clothed in, *vêtu de*
clothes, *les vêtements* m.; **peasant's —,** *les habits de paysan*
club (society), *le club*
club (for hockey), *la crosse*
coach, *le coche*
coal, *le charbon*
coast, *la côte*
coat, *l'habit* m., (overcoat) *le pardessus*
code, *le code*
coffee, *le café*
coin, *la pièce*
cold, *froid*; **be —,** (of people) *avoir froid*; **it is —,** (of weather) *il fait froid*
coldly, *froidement*
collection, *la collection*
college, *le collège*
come, *venir*
come back, *revenir, rentrer*
come down, *descendre*
come for a walk, *venir faire une promenade*
come forward, *s'avancer*
come home, *rentrer chez soi*
come in, *entrer*
come near (or 'nearer'), *s'approcher de*
come off, *se réaliser*
come out, *sortir*
come over, trans. *envahir*
come towards, *s'approcher de*
come up on, *monter sur*
come up to (a person), *aborder* + direct obj.
come upstairs, *monter*
comfort, *le confort*
comfortable, (of things) *confortable,* (of persons) **be —,** *être bien*

companion, *le compagnon, la compagne*
company, *la compagnie*
compartment, *le compartiment*
compete, *concourir*
complain, *se plaindre* ('about' or 'of' = *de*)
complainer, *le plaignant*
complaint, *la réclamation*
complete, adj. *complet*
complete, vb. *achever*
completely, *complètement*
comprehend, *comprendre*
conceal, *cacher*
conceited, *vaniteux*
concierge, *le* or *la concierge*
conclude, *conclure*
concrete, *le béton*
condescend, *daigner* ('to' = *de*)
conduct, *conduire*
conductor, *le conducteur*
confess, *avouer*
confusion, *la confusion,* Ex. XVIII, p. 72, *l'embarras* m.
consent, *consentir* ('to' = *à* + inf.)
consequence, in — of, *par suite de*
consider, *croire*
console, *consoler*
conspire, *conspirer*
Constable, *Monsieur l'Agent*
construct, *construire*
consult, *consulter*
contain, *contenir*
contents, *le contenu*
continent, *le continent*
continue, *continuer* ('to' = *à*)
contre-temps, *le contre-temps*
control, *maîtriser*
convenient, *opportun*
conversation, *la conversation*
convey, *porter*
convinced, *persuadé*
cook, *la cuisinière*
copy, *copier*
corner, *le coin*; **in the —,** *au coin*
cottage, *la chaumière*
cotton, *le coton*
cough, n. *la toux*
cough, vb. *tousser*
council chamber, *la chambre du conseil*
counter, *le comptoir*
country, *le pays,* (as opposed to the town) *la campagne*; **in or into the —,** *à la campagne*
country hotel, *l'hôtel de province*
country house, *le château*
countryside, *la campagne*
course (dish), *le plat*
course, in the — of the evening, *dans la soirée*
court, courtyard, *la cour*
cousin, *le cousin, la cousine*
cover, *couvrir*
covered with, *couvert de*
cow, *la vache*
creature, *la créature*
crier, *le crieur*
cross, be —, *être de mauvaise humeur*
cross, vb. *traverser,* (a bridge) *passer*
cross-roads, *les croisements de route*

crowd, *la foule*; **there is a —,** *il y a foule*; **in crowds,** *en foule*
crown, *la couronne*
crust, *la croûte*
cry, n. *le cri*
cry, vb. (exclaim), *s'écrier*
cry, vb. (shout), *crier*
cry (weep), *pleurer*; **— bitterly,** *pleurer à chaudes larmes*
cultivate, *cultiver*
cup, *la tasse*
cupboard, *l'armoire* f.
curiosity, *la curiosité*
curious, *curieux*; **be — to,** *être curieux de* + inf.
curiously, *avec curiosité*
curl, vb. *se retrousser*
curtain, *le rideau*
customer, *le client*
cut, cut off, *couper*
cut very thin, *très mince*

daisy, *la pâquerette*
daisy chain, *la guirlande*
damsel, *la damoiselle*
dance, *la danse*
danger, *le danger*
dangerous, *dangereux*
dare, *oser* (inf. without prep.)
dark, *noir*, (of weather) *sombre*; **it is —,** *il fait noir*
darling, *chéri(e)* (after noun)
daughter, *la fille*
day, *le jour, la journée*
daytime, in the —, *dans la journée*
dead tired, *brisé de fatigue*
deaf, *sourd*
deal, a good —, *beaucoup*
dear, *cher*; **my —,** (fem.) *ma chère*
debt, *la dette*
deceive, *tromper*
decide to, *décider de* + inf.
decision, *la décision*
decisive, *décidé*
decked with flags, *pavoisé*
declare, *déclarer*
deep, *profond*
deep bass, *gros, grosse*
delay, *le retard*
delicious, *délicieux*
delighted, *enchanté* ('to' or 'with' = *de*)
delightful, *ravissant*; **a — story,** *un conte charmant*
delivery (postal), *la distribution*
demonstrate, *démontrer*
depart, *partir*
departure, *le départ*
depend on, *dépendre de*
describe, *décrire*
deserted, *déserté*
desire, *désirer* + inf.
desk, *le bureau*
despair, in —, *au désespoir*
despatch, *expédier*
desperate, *prêt à tout*
destination, *la destination*
determined, be — that, *être décidé à ce que* + subj.
diamond, *le diamant*
die, *mourir*
difficult, *difficile*
difficulty, *la difficulté*; **have — in,** *avoir peine à* + inf.

dig, *bêcher*
din, *le vacarme*
dine, *dîner*
dining-room, *la salle à manger*
dinner, *le dîner*
direction, *la direction*
directly, conj. *dès que, aussitôt que*
disappear, *disparaître*
disappoint, *désappointer, décevoir*
discover, *découvrir*
discuss, *discuter*
disgraceful, *honteux*
disgusted, *dégoûté*
dismay, a look of —, *un air consterné*
disorder, *le mal*
distance, *la distance*
distinct, *distinct*
distinctly, *distinctement*
distress, in —, *en détresse*
district, *la région*
disturb, *déranger*
dive, *plonger*
diversion, *le divertissement*
do, *faire*
do good to, *faire du bien à*
do up, *fixer*
do without, *se passer de*
dock, in —, *au bassin*
doctor, *le médecin*
document, *le document*
dog, *le chien*
donkey, *l'âne* m.
door, *la porte*
dormouse, *le loir*
doubt, *le doute*
doubtless, *sans doute*
downstairs, *en bas*; **run —,** *descendre en courant*
dozen, *la douzaine*
dragon, *le dragon*
draw, draw aside, *tirer*
draw (with pencil), *dessiner*
draw out, *retirer* (Ex. XXVII, p. 93, *sortir*)
drawer, *le tiroir*
drawing-room, *le salon*
dreadful, *affreux* (in Ex. XXV, p. 91, before noun, otherwise after)
dreadfully, *affreusement*
dream, *rêver*
dress, n. *la robe*
dress, vb. trans. *habiller,* intrans. *s'habiller*
dressing-case, *la valise*
drink, *boire*
drive, n. *la promenade*; **go for a —,** *faire une promenade*
drive (a train), *conduire*
drive away *mettre à la porte*
drive right round, *contourner*
driver (of a car), *le chauffeur*; **engine —,** *le mécanicien*
drop, n. *la goutte*
drop, vb. *laisser tomber*
drum, *le tambour*
duchess, *la duchesse*
duck, *le canard*
during, *pendant*
dusty, it is very —, *il fait beaucoup de poussière*
duty, *le devoir*
dwell, *demeurer*

each, adj. *chaque*
eagerly, *l'air empressé*
early, adj. *prochain*
early, adv. *de bonne heure*; **— in the morning**, *de bon matin*; **very — in the day**, *très tôt dans la journée*
earth, *la terre*
easily, *facilement*
easy, *facile*
eat, *manger*
eau de Cologne, *l'eau de Cologne* f.
education, *l'éducation*
effort, *l'effort* m.; **make an — to**, *faire un effort pour* + inf.
egg, *l'œuf* m.
either, **not...either**, *ne pas... non plus*
elder, **eldest**, *aîné*
Eliza, *Élise*
emerge, *sortir*
empty-handed, *les mains vides*
end, *la fin*, (of a stick or table) *le bout*; **at the — of**, *au bout de* (but in Ex. XI, p. 67, *à la fin de*)
endeavour, *essayer* ('to' = *de* + inf.)
engage (room), *retenir*
engine, *la locomotive*, (of a car or aeroplane) *le moteur*
engine driver, *le mécanicien*
England, *l'Angleterre* f.
English, *anglais*
English women, *les Anglaises*
enjoy, *jouir de* (Ex. XX, p. 73, *trouver*)
enjoy oneself, *s'amuser*
enormous, *énorme*
enough, *assez*
enquire, *demander*
ensure, *assurer*
enter, *entrer* (*dans*)
enter for (a tournament), *se faire inscrire pour*
entertaining, *intéressant*
entirely, *entièrement*
entrance, *l'entrée*; **at the — to**, *à l'entrée de*
envelope, *l'enveloppe* f.
errand, **go out on an —**, *sortir faire une commission*
escape (make one's escape), *s'échapper*
escape from, *échapper à*
especially, *surtout*
even, *même* (invariable)
evening, *le soir*; **the — before**, *la veille au soir*; **in the course of the —**, *dans la soirée*
ever so many, *des quantités*
everybody, see **everyone**
every morning, *tous les matins*
everyone, *tout le monde*
every time, conj. *chaque fois que*
everything, *tout*
evident, *évident*
exact, *exact*, (of time) *précis*
exactly, *au juste*
examine, *examiner*
example, *l'exemple* m.; **for —**, *par exemple*
excellent, *excellent*
except, *sauf*
exchange for, *échanger pour* or *contre*

excited, *ému*
excitedly, *plein d'émoi*
exclaim, *s'écrier*
excursion, *la promenade*
excuse, n. *l'excuse* f.
excuse, vb. *excuser*
excuse me, *pardon*
exhausted, *épuisé*
exit, *la sortie*
expect, *attendre*; — **to,** *compter*
explain, *expliquer*
express, *l'express* m.
extraordinary, *extraordinaire*
extremely, *extrêmement*
eye, n. *l'œil* m.
eye, vb. *toiser*

face, *la figure*
fail to, *manquer de* + inf.
faint, *s'évanouir*
fair, *beau, belle*
fair (of hair), *blond*
fair sir, *beau sire*
fairly, *assez*
fairy, *la fée*
faithful, *fidèle*
fall, *tomber*
fall asleep, *s'endormir*
fall in, *tomber dedans*
fall to (begin to), *se mettre à*
family, *la famille*
famous, *célèbre*
fan, *l'éventail* m.
far, *loin*
far-away, adj. *lointain*
farm, *la ferme*
farmer, *le fermier*
farmer's wife, *la fermière*
fashion, *la mode*
fast, adj. *rapide*
fast, adv. *vite*
fast asleep, *profondément endormi*
fat, *gros et gras*
father, *le père*
fatiguing, *fatigant*
favour, *la faveur*
favourable, *avantageux*
fear, n. *la peur*
fear, vb. *craindre, avoir peur*; — **that,** see § 86; — **to,** *craindre de* + inf.
feeble, *faible*
feel, trans. *sentir*, intrans. *se sentir*
feel sorry that, *regretter que* + subj.
ferocious looking, *à l'air féroce*
fetch, *aller* or *venir chercher*; **go upstairs to —,** *monter chercher*
few, a —, *quelques*; **very —,** *très peu (de)*; **as — as,** *aussi peu de...que*
field, *le champ*
figure, *la forme*
fill, *remplir* ('with' = *de*)
finally, *enfin, finalement*
find, *trouver*
fine, *beau, belle*
finger, n. *le doigt*
finger, vb. *tâter*
finish, *finir*; — **doing,** *finir de faire*
fire, *le feu*
fire-place, *le foyer*
first, adj. *le premier*
first, adv. *d'abord*

fish, vb. *pêcher*
fisherman, *le pêcheur*
flame, *la flamme*
flight, *le vol*
flower, *la fleur*
fly, *voler*
flying squad, *la brigade volante*
fog, *le brouillard*
foggy, **in — weather**, see § 100
folk, **the —**, *les gens*
follow, *suivre*
following, *suivant*; **the — day**, *le lendemain*
fond, **be — of**, *aimer*; **be very — of**, *aimer beaucoup*; **be very — of doing**, *aimer beaucoup faire*
food, *la nourriture*
foot, *le pied*; **on —**, *à pied*
footstep, *le pas*
for, conj. *car*
for, prep. *pour*
for (during), (of past time) *pendant*, (of future time) *pour*
forbid (anyone to), *défendre* (*à quelqu'un de* + inf.)
foreign, *étranger*
foreigner, *l'étranger*
forest, *la forêt*
forget, *oublier* ('to' = *de* + inf.)
forgive, *pardonner* (*à*)
form, *la forme*, (telegraph) *la formule*
former, *ancien*
former (opposed to latter), *celui-là*, *celle-là*
fortnight, *quinze jours*, *une quinzaine*
fortune, *la fortune*
fountain pen, *le stylo*
France, *la France*
free, *libre*
French, *français*
French (language), *le français*
Frenchman, *le Français*
friend, *l'ami*, *l'amie*
fright, *la frayeur*; **die of —**, *mourir de peur*
frighten, *faire peur à*
frightened, **be —**, *avoir peur*
frightfully, *terriblement*
front, **in — of**, *devant*
front door, *la porte d'entrée*
frontier, *la frontière*
full, *plein*
fumble for, *chercher... à tâtons*
funny, *amusant*
furious, *furieux*
future, *l'avenir*

gain, *gagner*
gain height, *prendre de la hauteur*
gallery, *la galerie*
game, *la partie*; p. 67, *le jeu*
garage, n. *le garage*; **in the —**, *au garage*; vb. *mettre au garage*
garden, *le jardin*
garden gate, *la grille du jardin*
garments, *les vêtements* m.
gate, *la porte*
gather, intrans. (of a crowd) *se rassembler*
gay, *gai*

gaze at, *contempler*
gendarme, *le gendarme*
generally, *généralement*
gentleman, *le monsieur*
gentlemen's singles, *les simples messieurs*
gently, *doucement*
gents, *messieurs*
George, *Georges*
German, *allemand*
German (language), *l'allemand*
Germany, *l'Allemagne* f.
gesture, *le geste*
get, trans. *procurer*
get (to a place), *arriver*; **— there,** *y parvenir*
get (become), *devenir*
get at, *attraper*
get away, *partir*
get back, trans. *rattraper*
get cold, *refroidir*
get down, *descendre*
get home, *rentrer chez soi*
get hot, *chauffer*
get hungry, *avoir faim*
get in or into, *entrer* (*dans*), (of an aeroplane, car, taxi, train, etc.) *monter* (*dans*)
get into bed, *se coucher*
get late, *se faire tard*
get lighter, *faire plus clair*
get mixed up in, *s'empêtrer dans*
get out, trans. *sortir* (e.g. *sortir un passeport*)
get out of (aeroplane, car, coach, train, etc.), *descendre de*
get ready, *préparer*
get through to (on telephone), *se mettre en communication avec*
get tired, *se fatiguer*
get very tired of (doing), *se lasser de* (*faire*)
get to, *arriver à*
get up, *se lever*; **— — again,** *se relever*
get up on, *monter sur*
ghost, *le revenant*
ghost story, *une histoire de revenants*
giant, *le géant*
girl, *la jeune fille*; **little —,** *la petite fille*; **pretty —,** *la jolie fille*
give, *donner*
give back, *rendre*
give notice, *rendre son tablier*
give up, *renoncer à*
glad, content ('to' = *de* + inf.)
glade, *la clairière*
glance, n. *le regard*
glance at it, *y jeter un regard*
glance at one another, *se regarder*
glass, n. *le verre*
glass, adj. *de verre*
glasses (spectacles), *les lunettes* f.
gloomily, *d'un air maussade*
glove, *le gant*
glue, vb. *coller*
go, *aller*, (of a watch) *marcher*
go ahead, *aller tout droit*
go along (a road), *suivre*
go away, *s'en aller*
go back, *retourner*
go back into, *rentrer dans*

go by, *passer*
go down, *descendre*
go for (fetch), *aller chercher*
go for a walk, *aller se promener*
go for a long walk, *faire une longue promenade*
go home, *rentrer chez soi*
go in or **into,** *rentrer* (*dans*)
go near to, *s'approcher de*
go off, *partir*
go on, go on with, *continuer*
go on (doing), *continuer* (*à faire*); **she still goes on...,** *elle continue à*+inf.
go on better, *aller mieux*
go on board, *s'embarquer*
go out or **outside,** *sortir*
go out (of a fire), *s'éteindre*
go round, *faire le tour de*
go to bed, *aller se coucher*
go to sleep, *s'endormir*
go up or **upstairs,** *monter*
go up to, (a person) *aborder,* (a thing or place) *s'approcher de*
goal, *le but*
goal-keeper, *le gardien de but*
God, *Dieu*
gold, n. *l'or,* adj. *d'or*
golf, *le golf*
golf ball, *la balle de golf*
golf club (society), *le club de golf*
good, *bon, bonne*
good, do — to, *faire du bien à*
good, what is the — of, *à quoi bon*+inf.
good deal, a — —, *beaucoup*
good day, *bon jour*
good night, *bon soir*
good tempered, *de bonne humeur*
Government form, *la formule administrative*
governor, *le gouverneur*
gradually, *peu à peu*
grandfather, *le grand-père*
grandparents, *les grands-parents*
grass, *l'herbe* f. (Ex. XLV, p. 110, *le gazon*)
grateful, *reconnaissant*
grave, *la tombe*
gravel, *le sable*
great, *grand*; **a — deal, a — many,** *beaucoup*
Greenwich time, *l'heure de Greenwich*
greet, *saluer*
grey, *gris*
grieve, *attrister*
groan, *gémir*
ground, *la terre*; **on the —,** *par terre*
grow (become), *devenir*
grow anxious, *s'inquiéter*
growl, (of people) *grogner,* (of a dog) *gronder*
grumpy, *maussade*
guard, *surveiller*
guess, *deviner*
guest, *l'invité*(*e*)
guinea, *la guinée*
gun, *le fusil*

hair, *les cheveux*
half, adv. *à moitié*
half, an hour and a —, *une heure et demie*
half an hour, *une demi-heure*

half-crown, *la demi-couronne*
half empty, *à moitié vide*
half-time, *la mi-temps*
half-way to, *à mi-chemin de*
hall, *la salle,* (entrance hall) *le vestibule*
hallo! *allo!*
halt, *s'arrêter* (Ex. XLIV, p. 60, *faire halte*)
ham, *le jambon*
hand, n. *la main*
hand, on the other —, *d'autre part*
hand, — back, — over, *remettre*; **— in,** *donner*
handbag, *le sac à main*
handle, *la manivelle*
handsome, *beau*
hang, *pendre*
hang up (again), *raccrocher*
hanging from, *suspendu à*
hanging on, *accroché à*
happen, *arriver, se passer*
happily, *heureusement*
happy, *heureux* ('to' = *de* + inf.)
harbour, *le port*
hard, *dur*
hardly, *ne...guère*
hardly...anyone, *ne...presque personne*
harm, n. *le mal*; **not to do any — to,** *ne pas faire de mal à*
harm, vb. *faire mal à*
harness, *atteler*
hasten towards, *accourir vers*
hastily, *en hâte*
hat, *le chapeau*
hate, *détester*
haunted, *hanté*
have (a bath or meal), *prendre*; **— a thing done,** see § 60 (*c*)
have to, see *devoir*, § 54
head, *la tête*
health, *la santé*
heap, *le tas*
hear, *entendre*
hear that, *apprendre que*
heart, *le cœur*
heat, n. *la chaleur*
heat, vb. *chauffer*
hedge, *la haie*
Helen, *Hélène*
help, n. *le secours*
help (someone to do), *aider (quelqu'un à faire)*
help, he could not — doing, *il ne put pas s'empêcher de faire*
hen, *la poule*
here, *ici*
here comes, here is, *voici*
hesitate, *hésiter* ('to' = *à* + inf.)
hide, *cacher*
highwayman, *le voleur*
highly pleased, *bien content*
hill, *la colline*
himself, *lui-même*
hind legs, *les pattes de derrière*
his, *son, sa, ses*
hoarse, *enroué*
hockey, *le hockey*
hockey match, *le match de hockey*
hold, *tenir*
hold out, trans. *tendre,* intrans. *tenir*
hold up, *soutenir*
hole, *le trou*

holidays, *les vacances* f.
holly, *le houx*
home, *la maison*
hoot, *corner*
hope, n. *l'espoir* m.
hope, vb. *espérer*; **— to,** § 57
horizon, *l'horizon* m.
horn, *la trompe*
horn-blower, *le sonneur de trompe*
horror-stricken, *frappé d'horreur*
horse, *le cheval*
horse-back, on —, *à cheval*
host, *l'hôte* m.
hostess, *l'hôtesse* f.
hot, *chaud*; **be —,** (of people) *avoir chaud*; **it is —,** (of weather) *il fait chaud*
hotel, *l'hôtel* m.
hour, *l'heure* f.
house, n. *la maison*; **at, in** or **to my —,** *chez moi*
house, vb. *abriter*
household affairs, *les affaires du ménage*
housework, *le ménage*
how? (interrog.) *comment?* **— is George?** *comment va Georges?*
how! (exclam.) *que, comme,* see §§ 107–108
however, *toutefois, pourtant, cependant*
how long, *combien de temps*
howl, *hurler*
hunger, *la faim*
hungry, be —, *avoir faim*; **be very —,** *avoir très faim*
hunt down, *poursuivre*
hunting, n. *la chasse*
hurriedly, *en hâte*
hurry, be in a —, *être pressé*; **be in a great —,** *être très pressé*
hurry down (a passage), *suivre en courant*
hurry out of, *sortir en hâte de*
hurry to or **toward,** *se rendre en hâte à*
hurry up, *se dépêcher*
hurry up to, *accourir vers*
hurt, do — to, *faire mal à*; **not to do any — to,** *ne pas faire de mal à*
husband, *le mari*

idea, *l'idée* f.
idiot, *l'imbécile*
ignorant, *ignorant*; **be wholly — of,** *ignorer complètement*
ill, *malade*
imagine, *imaginer*
imitate, *imiter*
immediately, *tout de suite*
immensely, *immensément*
importance, *l'importance* f.
important, *important*
impossible, it is — to, *il est impossible de* + inf.
improbable, *invraisemblable*
improve, intrans. *s'améliorer*
improve oneself, *se former*
improvement, an — over, *un progrès sur*
impudence, *l'impudence* f.
in, into, *dans, en*; **— blue,** *en bleu*

in consequence of, *par suite de*
in fact, *de fait*
in front of, *devant*
in order to, *afin de* + inf.
in search of, *à la recherche de*
in spite of, *malgré*
in that case, *en ce cas-là*
in this (or that) **way,** *de cette façon*
in vain, *vainement*
inadvertently, *par mégarde*
incident, *l'incident* m.
inclined, to be — to, *avoir envie de* + inf.
incomprehensible, *incompréhensible*
indeed, *vraiment*
indignant, *indigné*
indignantly, *avec indignation*
indoors, *à la maison*
influenza, *la grippe*
inform, *prévenir*
information, *les renseignements*
ink, *l'encre* f.
inn, *l'auberge* f.
insatiable, *insatiable*
inside, prep. *à l'intérieur de*
inside, adv. *dedans*
instal, *installer*
instantly, *sur-le-champ*
instead of, *au lieu de*
instructions, *les instructions* f.
intelligent, *intelligent*
intend to, *avoir l'intention de*
interested, be — in, *s'intéresser à*
interesting, *intéressant*
interpreter, *l'interprète* m.
intolerable, *insupportable*
introduce, *présenter*
introduction, *la présentation*
inventor, *l'inventeur* m.
invitation, *l'invitation* f.
invite (someone to do), *inviter* (*quelqu'un à faire*)
island, *l'île* f.
Italian (language), *l'italien*
Italy, *l'Italie* f.

Jack, *Jeannot*
Joan, *Jeanne*
joke, *la plaisanterie*
journey, n. *le voyage*
journey, vb. *se rendre*
jousts, *les joutes* f.
jump, jump down, *sauter*; **— out of bed,** see § 104
jump up, *se lever d'un bond*
just, I have —, *je viens de* + inf.; **I had —,** *je venais de* + inf.; **to be — going to,** *être sur le point de* + inf.
just as (with finite verb), *au moment où*; **— — he was starting,** *au moment de son départ*
just in time to, *juste à temps pour* + inf.
just like, adj. *tout pareil à*
just now, *tout à l'heure*

keep, *garder*; (in a shop or restaurant) **do you —?** *avez-vous?*
keep...from, *empêcher...de* + inf.

keep away from, *écarter de*
keep company, *tenir compagnie à*
keep fine, *continuer à faire beau*
keep one's word, *tenir parole*
keep open, *tenir ouvert*
key, *la clef*
kick off, *se débarrasser de*
kill, *tuer*
kilometre, *le kilomètre*
kind, adj. *bon*; **be — to,** *être bon pour*
kind, n. *la sorte*; **a new —,** *un nouveau genre*; **all kinds,** *toutes sortes*
kindly, *veuillez*+inf.
kindness, have the — to, *avoir la bonté de*+inf.
king, *le roi*
kingdom, *le royaume*
kiss, vb. *baiser*
kitchen, *la cuisine*
knee, *le genou*; **fall on one's knees,** *tomber à genoux*
kneel down, *s'agenouiller*
knight, *le chevalier*
knock, *frapper*
know (a fact), **— that,** *savoir,* (be acquainted with) *connaître*
know about, *être averti de*
know how to, *savoir*+inf.
know nothing about, *ne rien entendre à*

lad, *le garçon*
lady, *la dame*; **young —,** *la jeune fille*
lady clerk, *l'employée*
lady player, *la joueuse*
laid up, *alité* ('with' = *de*)
lake, *le lac*
lamb, *l'agneau* m.
Lamb (Larry), *l'Agnelet*
lamp, *la lampe*
land, vb. *débarquer,* (of an aeroplane) *atterrir*
landlady, *la logeuse*
language, *la langue*
lantern, *la lanterne*
large, (of things) *grand,* (of people) *gros*
Larry the Lamb, *l'Agnelet*
last, *dernier*
last Christmas, *l'an dernier à Noël*
last night, *hier soir*
last week, *la semaine dernière*
late, adv. *tard*; **be —,** see § 111; **get —,** see 'get'
later, *plus tard*
latter, the —, *ce dernier, cette dernière*
laugh, vb. *rire* ('at' = *de*)
laughter, *les rires*
lay, lay down, *poser*
lead, *conduire,* (of a door or path or staircase) *mener*
lean, *s'appuyer*
leaning against, *appuyé sur*
leap to one's feet, *se lever d'un bond*
learn, *apprendre* ('to' or 'how to' = *à*+inf.)
learned, *savant* (in Ex. XXVIII, p. 51, before noun)
least, adj. *le* or *la moindre*

leave, n. *la permission* ('to' = *de*)
leave, trans. (person or place) *quitter*
leave, intrans. *partir*
leave (a thing to a person), *laisser*
leave behind, *laisser*
leave open, *laisser ouvert*
left, n. *la gauche*; **on the —,** *à gauche*
left, have no money —, see § 6
legacy, *le legs*
lend, *prêter*
less, adv. *moins*
lesson, *la leçon*
let (allow), *laisser*
let down, *baisser*
let fall, *laisser tomber*
let...know, *faire savoir, prévenir*
let through, *laisser passer*
letter, *la lettre*
library, *la bibliothèque*
lie, *mentir*
lie down, *se coucher*
life, *la vie*
lift, *lever*
light, n. *la lumière*; **by the — of,** *à la lumière de*
light, vb. *allumer*
lightly, *légèrement*
like, adv. *comme*
like, be —, *ressembler à*; **be very —,** *ressembler beaucoup à*
like, vb. *aimer*
like to, *vouloir*
likewise, *également*
line, *la ligne*
lip, *la lèvre*
liqueur, *le liqueur*
listen, *écouter*; **— to,** *écouter* + direct obj.
listener, *l'auditeur* m.
lit, *allumé*
lit up, *éclairé*
little, adj. *petit*
little, adv. *peu* (*de*); **a little,** *un peu*
live, *vivre*
live, live in (a place) *habiter*
lively, *vif, vive*
living, *vivant*
local, *du quartier*
local platform, *le quai de banlieue*
local train, *le train d'intérêt local*
lock, n. *la serrure*
lock, lock up, *fermer à clef*
locution, *la locution*
lodge, n. *le pavillon*
lodge a complaint, *faire une réclamation*
lodge at (an inn or hotel), *descendre à* or *dans*
lodging, *le logement*
London, *Londres*
lonely, *solitaire*
long, adj. *long*; **all day —,** *toute la journée*
long (a long time), *longtemps*
long, be — in, *tarder à* + inf.
longer, no —, *ne...plus*
longingly, *avec envie*
look, n. *le regard*; **a — of dismay,** *un air consterné*
look, look at, *regarder*

look astonished, gay, happy, uncomfortable, etc., *avoir l'air étonné, joyeux, heureux, gêné,* etc.
look after, *s'occuper de*
look down, *baisser les yeux*
look for, *chercher* + direct obj.
look forward to, *compter sur*
look out! *attention!*
look out for, *faire attention à*
look out of, *regarder par*
look sternly at, *fixer d'un regard sévère*
look through (the window), *regarder par (la fenêtre)*
look up, *lever les yeux*
loop the loop, *boucler la boucle*
lose, *perdre*
lose no time in, *ne pas tarder à* + inf.
lose the way, *se tromper de chemin*
lose time (of a train), *prendre du retard*
loss, *la perte*
lot, n. *le tas*; **a —,** *beaucoup*; **a — of men,** *un tas de gens*; **a — of children,** *un tas d'enfants*
loud, loudly, adv. *haut*; **play loudly,** *jouer fort*; **bark loudly,** *aboyer fort*
loud-speaker, *le haut-parleur*
love, *aimer*
lovely, *beau, belle*
loving, *affectionné*
low, *bas, basse*
luck, *la chance*; **what —!** *quelle veine!*
luggage, *les bagages* m.
lunch, n. *le déjeuner*; **have a good —,** *bien déjeuner* (vb.)
lunch, vb. *déjeuner*
lying, *posé*

ma'am, *madame*
machine, (aeroplane) *l'appareil* m., (bicycle) *le vélo* (Ex. XLVI, p. 111, *la machine*)
madam, *madame*
magician, *le sorcier*
magnificent, *magnifique*
maid, *la femme de chambre* (Ex. XXXVII, p. 56, *la bonne*)
main gate, *la porte principale*
make, *faire*
make + adj. (e.g. make happy), *rendre*
make a dash for, *ne faire qu'un saut jusqu'à*
make a mistake, *se tromper*
make a speech, *prononcer un discours*
make fun of, *se moquer de*
make one's way to, *se rendre*
make up one's mind to, *résoudre de* + inf.
mamma, *maman*
man, *l'homme*
manage, *s'en tirer*
manage to, *parvenir à, pouvoir*
manager, *le gérant*
manger, *la mangeoire*
manners, *les manières* f.
mantel-piece, *le manteau de la cheminée*
many other(s), *bien d'autres*

many things, see § 3 (*a*)
map, *la carte*
mark, *marquer*
married, *marié*
marry, *épouser*
marvellous, *merveilleux*
master, *le maître*
match, *l'allumette* f., (game) *le match*
mate, *l'époux* m.
matter, n. *l'affaire* f.
matter, for idioms connected with this word see § 112
mayor, *le maire*
meadow, *la prairie*
meal, *le repas*
mean, *vouloir dire*
meanwhile, *en attendant*
meet, *rencontrer*; **— each other**, *se rencontrer*
melt, *fondre*
member, *le membre*
merely, *ne...que*; **not —**, *non seulement*
merry, *gai*
metre, *le mètre*
mew, *miauler*
middle, *le milieu*; **in the — of**, *au milieu de*
midnight, *minuit*
mile, *le mille*
milk, *le lait*
milk-jug, *le pot au lait*
mind, vb. *faire attention à*
mind (that), *faire attention* (*à ce que* + subj.)
minute, *la minute*
miss, *manquer*
mist, *la brume*
mistake, n. *l'erreur* f.
mistake, make a —, *se tromper*
mistake the road, the castle, etc., *se tromper de chemin, de château*, etc.
mistletoe, *le gui*
mistress, *la maîtresse*, (of an inn) *la patronne*
mixed doubles, *les doubles mixtes*
mixed up, get — — in, *s'empêtrer dans*
modest, *modeste*
moisten, *mouiller*
moment, *le moment, l'instant*; **at that (or this) —**, *à cet instant*; **at any —**, *d'un moment à l'autre*
money, *l'argent* m.
month, *le mois*
more, *plus*; **— and —**, *de plus en plus*
moreover, *du reste*
morning, *le matin*, (in speaking of the weather) *la matinée*
most men, *la plupart des hommes*
most of (with a singular noun), *la plus grande partie de*
mother, *la mère*, (as a mode of address) *maman*
motor, vb. *voyager en auto*
motor-bicycle, *la moto-cyclette*
mount, vb. *monter*
mountain, *la montagne*
mouth, *la bouche*
move, *bouger*

movement, *le mouvement*
mud, *la boue*
mug, *la timbale*
murmur, *murmurer*
music, *la musique*
musician, *le musicien*
must, I —, you —, one —, etc., *il faut* + inf. Also see *devoir*, § 54 (*a*)
must I . . . ? *faut-il que* + subj.?
my, *mon, ma, mes*
myself, *moi-même*

name, *le nom*
native, *l'indigène* m.
naturally, *naturellement*
nature, *la nature*
near, adv. *près*
near, prep. *près de*
nearest, *le* or *la plus proche*
nearly, *presque*
neatly rolled, *bien roulé*
necessary, adj. *nécessaire*; **be —,** *falloir*; **it became —,** use past def. of *falloir*
necessity, *la nécessité*
neck, *le cou*
need, n. *le besoin*; **I have no — to,** *je n'ai pas besoin de* + inf.
need, vb. *avoir besoin de*; **he needs,** *il lui faut* + direct obj.
neighbour, *le voisin*
neighbouring, *voisin*
neither . . . nor, *ne . . . ni . . . ni*, see § 6 (*d*)
nephew, *le neveu*
nest, *le nid*
net, *le filet*
never . . . again, *ne . . . jamais plus*
new, *nouveau*, (of a car, railway, etc.) *neuf* (after noun)
news, *les nouvelles* f., (piece of news) *la nouvelle*
newspaper, *le journal*
next, adj. *prochain*; **— Saturday,** *samedi prochain*; **— year,** *l'année prochaine*; **— time,** *la prochaine fois*
next, adv. *puis, ensuite*
next, conj. *la prochaine fois que*
next day, *le lendemain*
next morning, *le lendemain matin*
nice, *gentil, joli*; **be — to,** *être aimable pour*; **a — ride,** *une bonne promenade*; **a — party,** *une bonne soirée*
niece, *la nièce*
night, *la nuit*
nightfall, at —, *à la tombée de la nuit*
nightingale, *le rossignol*
no, adj. *aucun*(*e*), see § 6 (*b*)
no doubt, *sans doute*
no longer, *ne . . . plus*
no matter, *n'importe*
nod, *faire un signe de tête* ('to' = *pour* + inf.)
noise, *le bruit*; **make a —,** *faire du bruit*; **make a dreadful —,** *faire un bruit affreux*
none whatever, *absolument aucun*(*e*)
nonsense, *la sottise*
noon, *midi*
Norman, *normand*

north wind, *le vent du nord*
nose, *le nez*
not at all, *pas du tout*
not...at all, *ne...point*
not yet, *pas encore*
note, *le billet*; **make a —,** *prendre une note*
note-book, *le carnet*
nothing, *ne...rien*; **— more,** *ne...rien de plus*; **— further,** *ne...plus rien*
notice, n. *l'affiche* f.
notice, give —, *rendre son tablier*
notice, take — of, *faire attention à*
notice, vb. *apercevoir, remarquer,* (followed by abstract noun) *s'apercevoir de*
notice that, *s'apercevoir que*
novel, *le roman*
now, adv. *maintenant*
now (that), conj. *maintenant que*
number, (quantity) *le nombre,* (numeral) *le numéro*
numbers (figures), *les chiffres* m.

obey, *obéir (à)*
oblige, *obliger*; **be obliged to,** *être obligé de* + inf.
observation, *l'observation* f.
observe, *observer, remarquer*
occasionally, *de temps en temps*
occupy, *occuper*
odd, *étrange*
of course, *naturellement*
offer, n. *l'offre* f.
offer, vb. *offrir (à quelqu'un de faire quelque chose)*
office, *le bureau*
officer, *l'officier* m.
officer in charge, *le commissaire*
often, *souvent*
oh, dear! *mon Dieu!*
old, *vieux, vieil, vieille*; **six years —,** *âgé de six ans*; **to be six years —,** *avoir six ans*
old (former), *ancien*
old man, *le vieillard*
older (of people), *plus âgé*
on, *sur*
on account of, *par suite de*
on purpose, *exprès*
on that side of, *de ce côté-là de*
on the other hand, *d'autre part*
on the way, *en route*
once, *une fois*
once more, *une fois de plus*
one, indef. pron. *on*
one, the — which, *celui qui*
one by one, *un(e) à un(e)*
one more, *encore un(e)*
only, adj. *seul*; **an — son,** *un fils unique*
only, adv. *seulement, ne...que*
open, trans. *ouvrir,* intr. *s'ouvrir*
opening, *l'ouverture* f.
opportunity, *l'occasion* f.
opposite, adv. *en face,* adj. *opposé,* prep. *en face de*
or, *ou*
orchestra, *l'orchestre* m.
order, n. *l'ordre* m.
order (someone to do), *ordonner* or *commander (à quelqu'un de faire)*
order (food), *commander*

orders, *les instructions* f.
other, *autre*
ought, see *devoir*, § 55
our, *notre, nos*
out (extinguished), *éteint*
out of doors, *dehors*
outside, adv. *au dehors,* prep. *en dehors de*
over, prep. *par-dessus* (in Ex. LII, p. 117, use *sur*)
over there, *là-bas*
overcoat, *le pardessus*
overcome, *bouleversé* (Ex. XXX, p. 96, *ému*)
overwhelmed with, *accablé de*
own, adj. *propre*
owner, *le propriétaire*

pace, *le pas*
pack, *emballer*
packet, *le paquet*
page, *la page*
pained, quite —, *très attristé*
painter, *le peintre*
pair, *la paire*
palace, *le palais*
pale, *pâle*
pale, turn —, *pâlir*
pale blue, *bleu pâle,* invar.
palm (of the hand), *la paume*
papa, *papa*
paper, *le papier*
parcel, *le paquet*
parent, *le parent*
park, *le parc*
parrot, *le perroquet*
part, *la partie*
part with, *se séparer*
particularly, *particulièrement*
partner, (tennis) *le* or *la partenaire,* (dance) *le cavalier*
party, *la soirée*; **children's —,** *la soirée enfantine*
pass, vb. *passer*; **— over,** *survoler*; **— through,** *traverser*
passage, *le couloir*
passenger, *le voyageur*
passer-by, *le passant*
passport, *le passeport*
pastrycook, *le pâtissier*
path, *le sentier*
pause, *le temps d'arrêt*
pavilion, *le pavillon*
pay, *payer*; **— attention to,** *faire attention à*; **— a visit to,** *faire visite à*
pay for, *payer* + direct obj.
peacefully, *paisiblement* (Ex. XIX, p. 85, *tranquillement*)
peasant, *le paysan*
peculiar, *bizarre*
peep into, *jeter un regard furtif sur*
peer through, *jeter un regard à travers*
peg, *la patère*
pen, *la plume*
pencil, *le crayon*
penny, *deux sous*; **a — bun,** *une brioche de deux sous*
pennyworth, a — of, *deux sous de*
people, *les gens,* also see § 113 (in Ex. IV, p. 63, *le peuple*)
perceive, *apercevoir*
perched, *perché*

perfectly true, *exact*
perform stunts, *faire des acrobaties*
perhaps, *peut-être,* see § 32
person, *la personne*
Peter, *Pierre*
pick, *cueillir*
pick up, *ramasser*
picture, *le tableau*
picturesque, *pittoresque*
piece, *le morceau*
piece of rudeness, *l'impolitesse* f.
pilot, *le pilote*
pink, *rose*
pipe, *la pipe*
pity, what a —! *quel dommage!*
place, n. *l'endroit* m.; **in the — where,** *à l'endroit où*
place (in a railway carriage), *la place*
place, take the — of, *prendre la place de*; **take my —,** *prendre ma place*
place, take —, *avoir lieu*
place, vb. *poser*
plague, *tourmenter*
plain, adj. *laid*
plan, *le projet*
platform, *l'estrade* f., (railway) *le quai*
play, *jouer*; **— tennis,** *jouer au tennis*
player, *le joueur, la joueuse*
plead, *supplier*
pleasant, *agréable*
please, *s'il vous plaît*
please, vb. *plaire à, faire plaisir à*
pleased, *content* ('with' or 'to' = *de*)
pleasure, *le plaisir*
plenty, *beaucoup*
plumber, *le plombier*
plum pudding, *le plum pudding*
pocket, *la poche*
point (of pencil), *le bout*
point, on the — of, *sur le point de* + inf.
point out to, *faire observer à*
point to, *montrer,* (of a watch) *marquer*
poke (one's head out of), *passer* (*la tête par*)
police, *la police*
policeman, *l'agent* (*de police*)
police station, *le commissariat de police*
polite, *poli*
politeness, *la politesse*
poor, *pauvre*
pop down, *disparaître dans*
pope's palace, *le palais des papes*
port, *le port*
portable set, *l'appareil portatif* m.
porter, *le porteur*
portrait, *le portrait*
possible, *possible*
post (goal), *le poteau*
post, vb. *mettre à la poste*
posted (stationed), *posté*
postman, *le facteur*
post office, *le bureau de poste*
pound, *la livre*
pour, pour out, *verser*
powerful, *puissant*
practice game, *la partie d'entraînement*

praise, *louer*
precaution, take the — to, *prendre la précaution de*
precious, *précieux*
prefer, *préférer* (with inf. § 57)
prepare, trans. *préparer,* intrans. *se préparer* (*à*)
presence of mind, *la présence d'esprit*
present, n. *le cadeau*
present, vb. *présenter*
present, be — at, *assister à*
presently, *bientôt, tout à l'heure*
pretend to, *faire semblant de* + inf.
pretty, adj. *joli*
pretty (fairly), adv. *assez*
prevent (from doing), *empêcher* (*de faire*)
previous, on the — evening, *la veille au soir*
price, *le prix*
priest, *le prêtre*
princess, *la princesse*
principal, adj. *principal*
principal, n. *le directeur*
prison, *la prison*; **in —,** *en prison*
prisoner, *le prisonnier, la prisonnière*
probably, *probablement*
proceed to, *se mettre à* + inf.
profession, *la profession*
professor, *le professeur*
prolong, *prolonger*
promise, *promettre* ('to' = *de* + inf.); **— someone to,** *promettre à quelqu'un de* + inf.
propeller, *l'hélice* f.
proposal, *la demande en mariage*
proprietor, *le propriétaire*
proud, *fier*
proudly, *fièrement*
provide with, *munir de*
province, *la province*
provisions, *les provisions* f.
public, n. *le public*
pull down, *baisser*
pull off (a hat), *ôter*
pull oneself together, *se remettre*
pull (out of), *tirer* (*de*)
Punch, *Polichinelle*
punctual, *exact*
punctually at three, *à trois heures précises*
pupil, *l'élève* m. or f.
purpose, on —, *exprès*
purr, *ronronner*
purse, *la bourse*
push, *pousser*
put, *mettre*
put away, *cacher*
put back, *remettre*
put in, *y mettre*
put on, *mettre*
put out (a light), *éteindre*
put out of, *passer par*
put right, *réparer*
puzzled, *embarrassé*

quarter (of a mile), *le quart* (*de mille*); **— of an hour,** *le quart d'heure*
queen, *la reine*
queer, *drôle*
question, *la question*; **it is a — of,** *il s'agit de*; **ask a —,** *poser une question* (*à*)

quick, quickly, adv. *vite*
quick, be —, *se dépêcher*
quiet, *tranquille*
quietly, *tranquillement*
quite, *tout à fait, tout,* see § 17 (g); **— close to, — near to,** *tout près de*; **— ready,** *tout prêt*
quite a number of, *bon nombre de* + plur. verb

rabbit, *le lapin*
rabbit hole, *le terrier*
rack, *le filet*
rails, *les rails* m.
railway carriage, *le compartiment de chemin-de-fer*
railway line, *la ligne de chemin-de-fer*
rain, vb. *pleuvoir*
raise, *lever,* (the hat) *ôter*
rapidly, *rapidement*
rather, *un peu*
razor, *le rasoir*
reach, *arriver à*
reach home (3rd pers. sing.), *arriver chez lui*
read, *lire*
reading, *la lecture*
ready, *prêt* ('to' = *à* + inf.)
real, *vrai*
realise, *comprendre*
really! exclam. *vraiment!*
really, adv. *réellement*
reappear, *réapparaître*
rear-light, *le feu arrière*
reason, *la raison*
reassured, *rassuré*
receive, *recevoir*
receiver (telephone), *le récepteur*
receiving set, *le poste récepteur*
recognise, *reconnaître*
red, *rouge*
reflect, *réfléchir*
refuse, *refuser* ('to' = *de* + inf.)
regard, *regarder, considérer*
regret, *regretter*
regretfully, *à regret*
relate, *narrer*
release, *dégager*
relentlessly, *sans pitié*
relief, *le soulagement*
remain, *rester*
remain silent, *garder le silence*
remark, n. *le propos*
remark, vb. *déclarer*
remarkable, *remarquable*
remedy, *le remède*
remember, *se souvenir de*; **— to,** *se souvenir de* + inf.
remind (a person of a thing), *rappeler* (*une chose à une personne*)
repair, *réparer*
repair to, *se rendre à*
repairs, *les réparations* f.
repeat, *répéter*
reply, n. *la réponse*; vb. *répondre*
request, *la requête*
request, vb. *recommander* (*à quelqu'un de faire quelque chose*)
resemble, *ressembler à*; **— each other,** *se ressembler*
resolve, *résoudre* ('to' = *de* + inf.)
responsible for, *responsable de*
rest, n. *le repos*
rest (remainder), n. *le reste*
rest, vb. *se reposer*

restaurant, *le restaurant*
restore, *rendre*
retort, *riposter*
return, n. *le retour*; **on his —,** *à son retour*; **— journey,** *le voyage de retour*
return (give back), *rendre*
return, (go back) *retourner,* (come back) *revenir*; **— home,** *rentrer, rentrer chez soi*
reveal, *révéler*
revolution, *la révolution*
revolver, *le revolver*
rhododendron, *le rhododendron*
rich, *riche*
ride, n. *la promenade*; **have a nice —,** *faire une bonne promenade*; **take someone for a —**; *faire faire une promenade à quelqu'un*
ride away, ride off, *s'en aller*
riding, *monté à*
right, on the —, to the —, *à droite*; **on my —,** *à ma droite*
right, be —, *avoir raison*
ring, *la bague* (Ex. IX, p. 79, *l'anneau* m.)
ring, ring the bell, *sonner*; **the bell rings,** *on sonne*
ring for, *sonner* + direct obj.
ring out, *retentir*
ring up (on telephone), *téléphoner à, donner un coup de téléphone à*
rise, rise to one's feet, *se lever*
risk it, *risquer le coup*
river, *la rivière*
Riviera, *la côte d'Azur*
road, *la route, le chemin*
rob (a person of a thing), *voler* (*une chose à une personne*)
robber, *le voleur*
robin, *le rouge-gorge*
roof, *le toit*
room, *la pièce, la salle,* (bedroom) *la chambre*
rough, *mauvais*
round, prep. *autour de*
round, n. (of golf) *le round*
row, *la rangée*
royalist, *le royaliste*
rub, *frotter*
rudeness, piece of —, *l'impolitesse* f.
ruffle, *contrarier*
ruined, *gâté*
run, *courir,* (of an engine) *marcher*
run (a distance), *faire . . . à pied*
run across, *traverser en courant*; **— along,** *parcourir*; **— away,** *se sauver*; **— back,** *retourner en courant*
run downstairs, run in, run out, see § 48
run up to, *courir vers*
rush, *se précipiter* ('to' = *vers*)
rush up to, *accourir vers*
Russian, *russe*

sad, *triste*
sadly, *tristement*
safe, adj.; **— and sound,** *sain et sauf*
safe, n. *le coffre-fort*
sail, n. *la voile*
sale, *la vente*
Salome, *Salomé*
salt, *le sel*

same, *le* or *la même*
satisfaction, *la satisfaction*
satisfied, *satisfait* ('with' = *de*)
satisfy, *satisfaire*
saucepan, *la casserole*
sausage, *la saucisse*
sausage machine, *la machine à saucisses*
save, *sauver*
sawdust, *la sciure*
say, *dire*; — **to oneself,** *se dire*
say rude things to, *injurier* + direct obj.
scan, *examiner*
scarcely, *à peine, ne...guère*
scene, *la scène*
scenery, *le paysage*
scent, *le parfum*
school, *l'école* f.
school friend, *un ami de collège*
scold, *gronder*; **be scolded,** *se faire gronder*
scoring card, *la carte pour marquer les points*
Scotland, *l'Écosse* f.
scowl, say with a —, *bougonner*
scratch, *gratter*
sea, *la mer*; **by —,** *sur mer*; **at —,** *en mer*
search, *la recherche*; **in — of,** *à la recherche de*; **a long —,** *de longues recherches*
search for, *chercher* + direct obj.
sea-sickness, *le mal de mer*
sea-side, *le bord de la mer*
sea-side town, *la ville balnéaire*
season, *la saison*
season ticket-holder, *l'abonné du chemin-de-fer* m.
seat, *la place*
seated, *assis*
second-hand, *d'occasion*
secret, *le secret*
secretary, *le secrétaire*
sedate, *rassis*
see, *voir*; — **again,** *revoir*
seeds, *les graines* f.
seem, *sembler, paraître*; **it seems to me,** *il me semble*
Seine, *la Seine*
seize, *saisir*
seized with, *saisi de*
select, *choisir*
sell, *vendre*
send, *envoyer*
send for, *faire venir*
sender, *l'envoyeur* m.
serious, *grave*
seriously, *d'un ton sérieux*
servant, *le* or *la domestique*, (of a farmer) *le valet*
serve, *servir*
set, (tennis) *la manche, le set,* (wireless) *l'appareil* m.
set, vb. (of the sun) *se coucher*
set about it, *s'y prendre*
set off or **out,** *partir*
set with (of a ring), *serti de*
several, *plusieurs*
sew, *coudre*
shade, in the —, *à l'ombre*
shake, *secouer*
shake with cold, *trembler de froid*
shameful, *scandaleux*
shave, intrans. *se raser*
sheet, *la feuille*
selfish, *égoïste*
shine, *briller*

shining (of rails), *luisant*
ship, *le bateau*
shoe, *le soulier*
shoot, *tirer*
shop, (large) *le magasin,* (small) *la boutique*
shop, vb. *faire des courses*
shopman, *le marchand*
short, *court*
shortly after, *peu de temps après, peu après*
shoulder, *l'épaule* f.
shout, *crier*; **— for help,** *crier au secours*
show, n. *le spectacle*
show, vb. *montrer*
shut, *fermer*; **— again,** *refermer*
shut up, *enfermer*
side, *le côté*; **by the — of,** *à côté de*; **on that — of,** *de ce côté-là de*; **on the other — of,** *de l'autre côté de*
sigh, n. *le soupir*
sigh, vb. *soupirer*
sight, (eyesight) *la vue,* (spectacle) *le spectacle*; **by the — of,** *à la vue de*
sign (to someone to), *faire signe* (*à quelqu'un de* + inf.)
signal, n. *le signal*
signal to, *faire signe à*
silent, *silencieux*; **keep** or **remain —,** *garder le silence*
silk, *la soie*
silly, a very — policeman, *un imbécile d'agent*
silver, adj. *d'argent, en argent*
silvery, *argenté*
since, conj. (because), *puisque*
since, adv. *depuis*
sing, *chanter*
sir, *monsieur*; **fair —,** *beau sire*
sister, *la sœur*
sister-in-law, *la belle-sœur*
sit, sit down, *s'asseoir,* see § 117
sit up, *se redresser*
sitting, *assis*
sitting-room, *le salon*
situated, *situé*
situation, *la situation*
skeleton, *le squelette*
skilful, *habile*
sky, *le ciel*
sky-scraper, *le gratte-ciel*
sleep, n. *le sommeil*
sleep, vb. *dormir*
sleepily, *d'un air endormi*
sleepy, be —, *avoir sommeil*; **be very —,** *avoir grand sommeil*
slice, (of bread and butter) *la tartine,* (of ham) *la tranche*
slightest, *le* or *la moindre*
slip, *glisser*
slip...through, *y glisser*
slipper, *la pantoufle*
slow, adj. *lent*
slow down, *ralentir*
slowly, *lentement*
small, *petit,* (in height, of people) *de petite taille*
smart, *chic*; **— people,** *les gens chics*
smile, n. *le sourire*
smile, vb. *sourire*; **— at,** *sourire à*
smoke, n. *la fumée*
smoke, vb. *fumer*
snatch up, *saisir*
snow, *la neige*

snub (someone), *mettre (quelqu'un) à sa place*
so + adj. or adv. *si*
so, and so, conj. *alors, donc*
so few, *si peu de*
so long as, *pourvu que* + subj.
so many, so much (quantity), *tant de*
so much, *tellement*
so that (in order that), *pour que* + subj.
soap, *le savon*
sob, n. *le sanglot*
sob, vb. *sangloter*
sofa, *le canapé*
soldier, *le soldat*
solo, *le solo*
some, *du, de la, des,* adj. *quelque(s),* pron. *en*
someone, *quelqu'un*
something, *quelque chose*
sometimes, *quelquefois*
son, *le fils*
song, *le chant*
soon, *bientôt*
soon after(wards), *peu après*
sorrow, *le chagrin*
sorry, be — to, *regretter de* + inf.; **be very or so — to,** *regretter beaucoup de* + inf.
sort, *la sorte*
sound, *le bruit*
south, invar. adj. *sud*; n. *le sud*
spade, *la bêche*
Spain, *l'Espagne* f.
Spanish, *espagnol*
spare the life of, *laisser la vie à*
spare the feelings, *ménager les susceptibilités*
spectacle, *le spectacle*
spectator, *le spectateur*
speech, *le discours*; **make a —,** *prononcer un discours*
speed, *la vitesse*
speedometer, *l'indicateur de vitesse*
spell, n. *le charme*
spend (time, etc.), *passer*
spirit, *l'esprit* m.
spiteful, *rancunier*
splendid, *splendide*
spot (place), *l'endroit* m.
spring, *le printemps*; **in —,** *au printemps*
spring (of a toy engine), *le ressort*
spring to the ground, *sauter à terre*
spy, *l'espion, l'espionne*
stable, *l'écurie* f.
stage, (theatre) *la scène,* (coach) *le relais*
staid, *posé*
staircase, *l'escalier* m.
stale, *fade*
stamp, *le timbre*
stand, (of people and animals) *se tenir (debout),* (of things) *se trouver*
stand out against, *se découper sur*
stand up, *se relever*
start, *partir* ('for' = *pour*)
start going, trans. *mettre en marche*
start off again, *repartir*
start out, *se mettre en route*
start to one's feet, *se lever d'un bond*

start up (an engine), *mettre en marche*
startle, *faire tressaillir*
state, *l'état*
station, (large) *la gare,* (small) *la station*
station (wireless), *le poste*
station-master, *le chef de gare*
stationed, *placé*
stay, *rester*
stay in bed, *garder le lit*
steal, *voler* (*une chose à une personne,* see § 18)
steamer, *le vapeur*
steel, *l'acier* m.
stentorian, in — tones, *d'une voix de stentor*
step, *le pas*
sternly, *d'un air sévère*; **look —,** see **look**
stick, *la canne*
stifling, *étouffant*
still, *encore, toujours*
stir, — a foot, *bouger d'un pied*
stocking, *le bas*
stone, n. *la pierre,* adj. *de pierre*
stop, n. *l'arrêt* m.
stop, trans. *arrêter,* intrans. *s'arrêter*; — (doing), *cesser de* (*faire*)
storey, *l'étage* m.
storm, (of wind and rain) *la tempête,* (thunderstorm) *l'orage* m.
story, *le conte, l'histoire* f.; **tell a —,** *conter une histoire*
straight, adj. *droit*
straight, adv. *directement*
strange, *étrange*
stranger, *l'étranger* (*-ère*)
stream, n. *le ruisseau*
stream, vb. *ruisseler*
street, *la rue*
stretch out, *tendre*
strict, be very — about, *être très sévère pour*
stride rapidly towards, *s'approcher de...à grandes enjambées*
strike, *cogner,* (of a clock) *sonner*
stroke, *le coup*
strong, *fort*
struck with, *saisi de*
student, *l'étudiant* m.
study, n. *le bureau*
study, vb. *étudier*
stuff, vb. *fourrer*
stunts, *les acrobaties* f.
stupid, *bête*; **very —,** *bien bête*; **— cat,** *bête de chatte*
subject, *le sujet*
subside, *se calmer*
substitute, *le remplaçant*
succeed, *réussir*; **— in,** *réussir à* + inf.
successful, be — in, *réussir à* + inf.
such, (with adj.) *si,* (with noun) *un tel,* see § 17 (*d*)
suddenly, *tout à coup, subitement*
suffer, *souffrir*
suffering, *la souffrance*
suit, *le complet*; **in a blue —,** *en costume bleu*

summer, *l'été* m.; **in —,** *en été*; **a — day,** *une journée d'été*; **— holidays,** *les grandes vacances*
summit, *le sommet*
summon, *appeler*
sun, *le soleil*
sunk in slumber, *plongé dans le sommeil*
sunny, *ensoleillé*
sun-rise, *le lever du soleil*
sun-set, *le coucher du soleil*
supper, *le souper*; **have —,** *souper* (vb.)
supper-room, *le buffet*
supper-time, *l'heure du souper*
suppose, *supposer*
supposed, *prétendu* (before noun)
sure, *sûr*; **I'm —,** *j'en suis sûr*; **be — to,** *être sûr de* + inf. (Ex. L, p. 115, *ne pas manquer de*)
surprise, n. *la surprise*
surprise, vb. *surprendre*
surprised to, *surpris de* + inf.
surrender, *se rendre*
surround, *entourer* ('with' or 'by' = *de*)
survey, n. *l'examen* m.
survive, *survivre*
suspicion, *le soupçon*
suspiciously, *d'un air soupçonneux*
swan, *le cygne*
swim, *nager*
swimming pool, *le bassin de natation*
switch on the light, *rallumer l'électricité*
Switzerland, *la Suisse*
sympathy, *la sympathie*
system, *le système*

table, *la table*
table-cloth, *la nappe*
tail, *la queue*
take, *prendre* ('from' = *à*)
take (a person to a place), *conduire, amener*
take (a thing to a person or place), *porter*
take a walk, *faire une promenade* (*à pied*); **take someone for a ride, trip,** or **walk,** *faire faire une promenade à quelqu'un*
take back from, *reprendre à*
take care of, *prendre soin de*
take care to, *avoir* or *prendre soin de* + inf.
take care not to, *se garder bien de* + inf.
take home, *reconduire*
take into (a bedroom), *faire monter dans* (*une chambre*)
take off, trans. *ôter*
take off, intrans. (of an aeroplane) *décoller*
take out of, *tirer de*
take place, *avoir lieu*
tale, *le conte*; **tell a —,** *conter une histoire*
talk, *parler* ('about' = *de*), *causer*
task, *la tâche*
taste, *le goût*
taxi, in a —, *en taxi*
tea, *le thé*
team, *l'équipe* f.
tea-party, *le thé*
tea-pot, *la théière*

tea-shop, *le salon de thé*
tear down or **up,** *arracher*
tears, *les larmes* f.
teeing ground, *le tertre de départ*
telegram, *la dépêche*
telegraph form, *la formule télégraphique*
telephone, n. *le téléphone*
telephone, vb. *téléphoner*
telephone girl, *la téléphoniste*
telephone message, *le message téléphonique*
telephone service, *le service des téléphones*
tell, *dire*; — **each other,** *se dire*; — **someone to,** *dire à quelqu'un de*+inf.; — **a story** or **tale,** *conter une histoire*
temper, bad —, *la mauvaise humeur*
tempt, *tenter*
tenderly, *d'une voix tendre*
tennis, *le tennis*; — **tournament,** *le tournoi de tennis*
terminus, *le terminus*
terrible, *terrible*
terribly, *terriblement*
terrified, *effrayé*
thank, *remercier* ('for' = *de*)
thank you for, *merci de*
thanks, *les remerciements* m.
thanks, *merci*; — **very much,** *merci beaucoup*
that, adj. *ce,* (*cet*), *cette, ces*
that, indef. pron. *cela*
that, conj. *que*
that (one), *celui-là, celle-là*
theatre, *le théâtre*
their, *leur, leurs*
then, *alors, donc,* (next) *puis, ensuite*
there, *là, y*
there he is, *le voilà*
there is (the house), *voilà* (*la maison*)
there you are! *voilà!*
therefore, *donc*
thereupon, *sur ce*
thick, *épais*
thief, *le voleur*
thin, cut very —, *très mince*
thing, *la chose*
think, *croire, penser, trouver*; **don't you — so?** *ne trouvez-vous pas?*
think of, (reflect on) *penser à,* (have an opinion about) *penser de*
thirsty, be —, *avoir soif*; **be very —,** *avoir très soif*
this, adj. *ce* (*cet*), *cette, ces*
this, pron. (opposed to that), *ceci*
this (one), *celui-ci, celle-ci*
thither, *y*
thorn bush, *le buisson d'aubépine*
though, *bien que, quoique,* see § 90 (*b*)
thought, *la pensée*
thoughtfully, *d'un ton pensif*
threaten (someone with), *menacer* (*quelqu'un de*)
threaten to, *menacer de*+inf.
through, *à travers*
throw, throw aside, *jeter*
throw down, *jeter à terre*
thus, *ainsi*
ticket, *le billet*

tie, *la cravate*
tied fast, *solidement attaché*
tight (of shoes), *petit*
till, prep. *jusqu'à,* conj. *jusqu'à ce que* + subj.
time, *le temps*; **from — to —,** *de temps en temps*; **at the same —,** *en même temps*; **have — to,** *avoir le temps de* + inf.
time (of day), *l'heure* f.; **what — is it?** *quelle heure est-il?*
time (occasion), *la fois*; **this —,** *cette fois*
timid, *timide*
tired, *fatigué*; **get —,** *se fatiguer*; **get very — of,** *se lasser de*; **be — of,** *s'ennuyer de*
tire out, *épuiser*
tiresome, *ennuyeux*
tiring, *fatigant*
to, prep. *à*
to (in order to), *pour* + inf.
tobacco, *le tabac*
today, *aujourd'hui,* **— week,** *d'aujourd'hui en huit*
together, *ensemble*
tomato sandwiches, *les sandwichs à la tomate*
tomorrow, *demain*
tone, *le ton*
too, too many, too much, *trop (de)*
too (also), *aussi*
tooth, *la dent*
top, *le sabot*
tortoise, *la tortue*
touch, *toucher*
tournament, see **tennis**
towards, *vers*
town, *la ville*; **in** or **to —,** *en ville*
town-crier, *le crieur public*
town-hall, *l'hôtel de ville*
toy, *le jouet*
Toytown, *Joujouville*
track, *la voie*
tradesman, *le marchand*
traffic signs, *les signaux lumineux*
train, *le train*; **by —,** *par le train*
translate, *traduire*
transmission, *l'émission* f.
travel, *voyager*
traveller, *le voyageur*
treacherous, *traître* (before noun)
tread on, *appuyer sur*
tree, *l'arbre* m.
tree-trunk, *le tronc d'arbre*
tremendous, it's a — success, *ça marche à merveille*
trim, vb. *rafraîchir*
trip, n. *la promenade*; **take for a —,** *faire faire une promenade à (quelqu'un)*
trouble, be in —, *être dans la peine*
troubled, *inquiet*
troubles, *les maux* m.
troublesome, *ennuyeux*
trumpet, *la trompette*
truth, *la vérité*
try, *essayer*
try to, (attempt to) *essayer de,* (make an effort to) *tâcher de*
tunnel, *le tunnel*
turn, *le tour*; **in —,** *à tour de rôle*; **in her —,** *à son tour*
turn, trans. *tourner,* intrans. *se tourner* ('to' or 'towards' = *vers*)

turn inside out, *retourner*
turn into, trans. *changer en*
turn off, *arrêter, fermer*
turn over, *retourner*
turn pale, *pâlir*
turn round, *se retourner,* (of a car) *tourner*
turn up, *se présenter*
turning, *le tournant*
twice, *deux fois*
twilight, *le crépuscule*

ugly, *laid* (after noun)
umbrella, *le parapluie*
unable to, *ne pouvant*
uncle, *l'oncle*
uncomfortable, *gêné*
under, prep. *sous*
understand, *comprendre*
undress, *se déshabiller*
uneasy, *inquiet*
unfortunately, *malheureusement*
unhappy, *malheureux*
unhook, *décrocher*
unless, *à moins que...ne,* §90 (*d*)
unlock, *ouvrir*
unmoved, *impassible*
unnecessary, *peu nécessaire*
unpleasant, *désagréable*
until, prep. *jusqu'à,* (after a negative) *avant*
until, conj. *jusqu'à ce que* + subj.
upon, *sur*
upstairs, *en haut*; **come or go —,** *monter*
up there, *là-haut*
urgent, *urgent*
use, what is the — of (doing)?, *à quoi bon* + inf.?; **what is the — of a book?** *à quoi sert un livre?*
use, *se servir de, employer*
used, be — to, *avoir l'habitude de*
useless, *inutile*
usher, *l'huissier* m.
usual, *habituel*
usually, *d'habitude*
utmost, the —, *le plus grand*
utter, *prononcer*

vain, adj. *vaniteux*
vain, in —, *vainement*
valley, *la vallée*
variety, *la variété*
velvet, *le velours*
vengeance, *la vengeance*
very, adv. *très*
very, adj., **the — clock,** *la pendule même*; **the — same,** *identiquement le* (or *la*) *même*
very much, *beaucoup* (never use *très beaucoup*)
vex, *vexer*
victim, *la victime*
view, *la vue*
village, *le village,* adj. *du village*
visible, *visible*
visit, n. *la visite*
visit, vb. (a place) *visiter,* (a person) *faire visite à*; **— again,** *revoir*
visitors, *les visiteurs,* (in a hotel) *les clients*
voice, *la voix*

wag, *le farceur*
waistcoat, *le gilet*
wait, *attendre*

wait for, *attendre* + direct obj.
wait till, *attendre que* + subj.
waiter, *le garçon*
waiting-room, *la salle d'attente*
waitress, *la serveuse*
wake, wake up, trans. *réveiller*, intrans. *se réveiller*
walk, a —, *une promenade*, (walking) *la marche*; **go for a —,** *faire une promenade (à pied)*
walk, vb. *marcher*; **— away,** *s'en aller*; **— back,** *rentrer à pied*; **— down,** *arpenter*; **— through,** *se promener par*; **— up and down,** *se promener de long en large*
wander, *errer*
want, *vouloir*; **I —, he wants,** etc., *il me faut, il lui faut*, etc.; **what you — is,** see § 16 (*a*)
want to, *vouloir*
warden, *le gardien*
wardrobe, *l'armoire* m.
warm, adj. *chaud*; **be —,** (of people) *avoir chaud*; **it is —,** (of weather) *il fait chaud*
warm, trans. vb. *réchauffer*
warm oneself, *se réchauffer*
warm one's hands, *se chauffer les mains*
warn, *avertir* ('to' = *de* + inf.)
wash, intrans. *se laver*
watch, n. *la montre*
watch, vb. *regarder*
watch for, *guetter*
water, *l'eau* f.
way (manner), **in that —,** *de cette façon*; **the only — to,** *le seul moyen de*; **in the — of,** *comme*
way (road), **on our —,** *en route* ('to' = *pour*)
wear, *porter*
weather, *le temps*; **the — is cold,** *il fait froid*; **it is awful —,** *il fait un temps affreux*
week, *la semaine*; **in a —,** *dans huit jours*
week-end, *le week-end*
weep, *pleurer*; **— bitterly,** *pleurer à chaudes larmes*
weight, *le poids*
well, adj. (in health) *bien portant(e)*
well, adv. *bien*
well!, exclam. *eh, bien!*
well-dressed, *bien habillé, bien mis*
well-informed, *instruit*
wet, *mouillé*
what? (what did you say?) *comment?*
what? pron. *qu'est-ce qui?*
what, adj. *quel*
what for? *pourquoi?*
wheel, n. *la roue*
wheel, vb. *amener*
wheel back, *ramener*
when? *quand? à quelle heure?*
when, relat. *quand, lorsque*
whenever, *lorsque, chaque fois que*
where? *où?*
whether, *si*
which, which one? *lequel?*
which way? *par où?*
while, conj. (temporal) *pendant que*, (on the other hand) *tandis que*
whiskers, *les moustaches* f.

whisper, in a —, *à voix basse*
whisper, vb. *chuchoter*
whistle, n. *le coup de sifflet*
white, *blanc*
whither, *où*
whole, the — month, *tout le mois*; **the — page,** *la page entière*
wholly ignorant, be — — of, *ignorer complètement*
why? *pourquoi?*
why not? *pourquoi pas?*
wide (of a hat), *à larges bords*
widow, *la veuve*
wife, *la femme*
wild, *sauvage*
willing, be —, *vouloir*
wind, n. *le vent*
wind, wind up, *remonter*
window, *la fenêtre*
windy, it is —, *il fait du vent*
wine, *le vin*
winter, *l'hiver* m.
wipe one's forehead, *s'essuyer le front*
wire (telegram), *la dépêche*
wire grating, *le grillage*
wireless, *la T.S.F.*
wireless set, *l'appareil de T.S.F.*
wish, *vouloir, désirer*
wit, *l'esprit* m.
with, *avec*
withdraw, *retirer*
within, *dans*
without, *sans*
witty, *spirituel*
woman, *la femme*
wonder, vb. *se demander*
wonderful, *merveilleux*
wood, *le bois*
wood-cutter, *le bûcheron*
wooden, *de bois, en bois*; **a — platform,** *une estrade en bois*
woodman, *le bûcheron*
word, *le mot*
work, n. *le travail*
work, vb. *travailler*, (of an engine or spring) *marcher*
worker, workman, *l'ouvrier* m.
world, *le monde*
worry, *s'inquiéter* ('about' = *de*)
worth, be —, *valoir*
worth while, it is — — (doing), *il vaut la peine de* + inf.
wrap, *envelopper*
wrath, *la colère*
wring one's hands, *se tordre les mains*
write, *écrire*
wrong (of a number), *mauvais*

yard (courtyard), *la cour*
yard (measure), *le mètre*
year, see § 116
yellow, *jaune*
yesterday, *hier*
yet, conj. *pourtant*
yet, not...yet, *ne...pas encore*
yonder, *là-bas*
you, *vous*, (familiar) *tu*
young, *jeune*
young lady, *la jeune fille*
your, *votre, vos*, (familiar) *ton, ta, tes*
yours, *le vôtre, la vôtre, les vôtres*
youth, *la jeunesse*

For EU product safety concerns, contact us at Calle de José Abascal, 56–1°, 28003 Madrid, Spain or eugpsr@cambridge.org.

www.ingramcontent.com/pod-product-compliance
Ingram Content Group UK Ltd.
Pitfield, Milton Keynes, MK11 3LW, UK
UKHW012328130625
459647UK00009B/135

* 9 7 8 1 3 1 6 6 0 1 7 4 7 *